All Will Be Well

AJ Holland

© AJ. Holland 2016

The photographs in this book are from Kirra SLSC 100 years by Peter D Kelly. Published in 2016 by CopyRight Publishing Company Pty Ltd.

Republished in 2024 by Crystal Voyager Press.

ISBN: 978-0-6486198-1-9

Peter Kelly is a friend of the author, Allan Holland, and has given permission for the photos to be used in All Will Be Well.

Contents

Introduction v

Chapter 1: Soxy and Choc 1
Chapter 2: Big Decisions 19
Chapter 3: Uncharted Waters 35
Chapter 4: A Whole New Life 57
Chapter 5: Vigilance and Service 1945 75
Chapter 6: Roy and Judith 97
Chapter 7: Life On the Beach 113
Chapter 8: Roy and Jude Are Well Into Their Journey 125
Chapter 9: Living the Family Dream 143
Chapter 10: Carina Pool 155

Afterword and acknowledgements 165

Introduction

When I was a young lad of just eleven, living in a small family home in Cannon Hill, which was then on the outskirts of Brisbane, I started my working life. My father had first settled in the area way back in 1915. He pitched a tent on two blocks of land he'd purchased for ten shillings each, put his belongings in the tent and went off to fight in France. Luckily, he came home, and even more fortunately, he brought back a war bride—my mum, Minnie. Over the years that followed they had five kids together, an achievement which entitled my dad to five days' work a week—one day for each child.

After World War II, the Australian government designed an incentive to replenish the depleted population. Families were encouraged to have as many babies as possible to help rebuild the country after the war that was to end all wars. Australia's losses were huge, and with a population before the war of just five million, we had lost 60,000 of our breeding stock as a nation. Lucky for me then there are five days in a week, as I might not ever have been born. You see, I was the fifth Holland child, with three older brothers and an older sister.

Chapter 1

Soxy and Choc

On this, my first ever day of paid work, I was excited about the chance to earn some money, and felt at last that I had a purpose—work, earn, own a horse. Of course, I was officially still at school, but I hoped that if I worked hard on this first job, I might be able to get away from school. I hated it so much. My job today was to help move 110 head of cattle from the sale yards just down the road from where I lived in Muir Street, to Samford, our droving destination for tonight. As I jumped up on top of my horse, Ginger, Mum called out to my brothers—Ernie, Tom and Harold—and my sister Rita to come and say goodbye. I felt important, but as usual, they all gave me a bit of stick, me being the youngest and all; all except Harold. He and I were very close. I looked over and saw Mum looking a bit anxious.

'Bye Mum. I'll be back tomorrow, don't know what time. Wish me luck, Mum.'

'I do, Roy. Make sure that you do exactly what you are told. Mr Lawler can get a bit cross if you don't listen.'

'I will, Mum.'

Ginger was all tacked up with the saddle that came with her when I bought her from Mr Porter, the milkman, for ten shillings, to be paid off at one shilling a week. Harold opened the gate for me and Ginger to get out of our front yard and on our way. As she went through the narrow open gate, she gave a little pig root. She hated gates and tight spots after her incident with the milk cart. If I hadn't come along, Mr Porter would have sent Ginger to the knackery. That's a one-way street. She had no idea of how lucky she was.

As I headed down Muir Street to Wynnum Road I had to be careful of morning traffic heading into town. The gates at the railway station crossing were across, and the gateman was standing, waiting for the steam train pulling four carriages to stop and allow passengers to get off and on. As the train started its huff and puff, Ginger started to get a bit twitchy. *She'll have to get used to all of these noises if she's going to be being a stock horse around here,* I thought to myself. After all, Cannon Hill is the end of the road for livestock in this corner of Queensland, so a stock horse needs to work in ways that are quite different from a horse pulling a dairy cart.

As Ginger and I waited at the closed gate waiting for the train to move on I could see the sale yards in full view to my right and the Redbank Abattoir straight ahead of me, its smoke stacks billowing thick white smoke. The train had gone far enough down the line, so the gateman swung open the gate, and we were off. Ginger was careful to not stand on the railway lines. She must have pulled the milk cart over this crossing before and would have learnt that horses' hooves and steel rail lines are a dangerous and slippery combination.

At the gates of the sale yards, I got down and led Ginger into the mustering area in front of the stockmen's quarters. It was a grand building—weatherboard and wide verandas all the way round. It was where all business was carried out for the sale yards. There was a beautiful tree in the centre of the mustering area.

It was now mid-morning, and January is the middle of summer here in Brisbane, so I took Ginger under the tree to get some comfort from the blistering sun. We wouldn't be leaving till four o'clock that arvo, and Mr Lawler had not turned up yet, so I thought I would sit down and lean against a stump conveniently left under the tree. Well, the next thing, I was woken up by a short fat man with a big straw hat. He was carrying on something fierce, pointing up into the tree. I couldn't help but notice a lot of plum seeds lying on the ground around Ginger. Turns out, the tree was the pride and joy of the little fat man and while I was asleep, Ginger had eaten all of the plums in the tree; there were only a few left. Now, I don't know much about plums and horses, but what I do know is that plums and horses don't go well together. They get the worst wind. That reaction had not started yet, but I could already hear some weird sounds coming from Ginger's gut.

Eventually the yelling stopped, and the gardener led me to the other side of the tree, pointing at a sign which read: 'No Horses'. Oops, bad start. I took Ginger over to the trough so she could have a drink. Hopefully, Mr Lawler would not find out. One thing for sure, I was not going to tell him. I was also a bit concerned about how I would explain all the farting that Ginger would be producing all the way to Samford, so I moved Ginger over to the other side of the yard, trying to distance myself as far away from the plum tree as was possible, but there are not many places to hide in a large dirt yard with nothing else in it.

Not long after, another stockman arrived. He had driven his Chevy truck to the sale yards and parked outside the mustering yard. The man had three kelpies with him—two older dogs and one younger dog. As they came past me, I said, 'Gooday, mate.'

'And good day to you, young fella.'

The two older dogs were giving the younger dog a hard time and the pup was cowering badly. Out of the blue, the stockman said, 'Hey lad, do you want a dog?'

'Which one?'

'The young one. He's not getting a fair go; keeps losing his confidence.'

As he finished explaining things, the young kelpie came over and sat on my foot. Where do you go from there?

'Can I have his collar?'

'Yep no problems.'

'What's his name?'

'He hasn't got one.'

The dog didn't move. He just stayed put, on my foot, looking up at me.

I thanked the stockman, and assured him that I would take good care of my new dog. He replied that he knew I would by the way I kept my horse and tack.

'Thank you,' I said.

Well, now I suddenly had a horse and a dog. I wondered what Mum would say. But first, he needed a name. Name, name, name, he has got to have a name. I liked chocolate and he was chocolate brown. *How about Choc?* I tried it out. Funny thing, he liked it. Any short, quick name works. He especially liked it when I gave him a crust from the sandwiches that Mum had slipped in my saddle bag.

A great thing about Mum; she always had a pressure cooker at full bore working its magic on a piece of silverside or a rooster that outstayed his welcome. There's nothing better than silverside on homemade wholemeal bread, especially with pickles. Mum was a little Yorkshire woman when my father married her. He was a proud Yorkshireman who fought on the

Somme in France in the First World War as a sapper. A sapper's job was to go forward in the darkness and hand-dig forward trenches. Terrifying when you think of it. I can't think of a more dangerous job.

A little later, Mr Lawler rode into the yard with his two kelpies, Mitch and Gracey. I didn't see him at first, as I was so busy playing with Choc. He opened the gate while he was still in the saddle of his horse, Daniel, a sixteen-hand chestnut stock horse with a beautiful white blaze on his forehead. Daniel had a lot of self confidence in his stance; helped by the fact that his owner was certainly one of the most respected horsemen in our area who commanded great respect from all who came into his life. He didn't say much, but when he did say something, you knew that he had thought carefully about it. He was always dressed for the job too: immaculate, stockwhip at the ready.

He dismounted. 'Hi there, Roy. Nice dog. Where did he come from?'

'His name is Choc. A stockman gave him to me a couple of hours ago because his older dogs were giving him hell, stopping his development.'

'Well, let's see how he goes. There's a pen of steers up that laneway. Let's see how much savvy he has.'

He tied Daniel to the fence and ordered Mitch and Gracey to stay. They knew that 'stay' meant stay. Choc didn't leave my side; we had an instant connection and trust. Or maybe Choc hadn't forgotten Mum's crust.

'Hop in the pen, Roy. Just walk around the cattle and see his reaction.'

A certain steadiness came over Choc who had a patient stare and seemed to understand pressure. Mr Lawler was satisfied with Choc's work and he gave his okay with Choc being at my side during the long drove in front of us.

'Well Roy, let's get back to our horses. Make sure you water Ginger and don't forget to fill your own saddle bottle. Have you got food?'

'Yes sir, Mum made me some corned beef and pickle sandwiches; that will do the trick.'

'I am going to go and get our charge sheet—a hundred and ten head of scrubbers.'

'What are scrubbers sir?'

'Cattle that have come off poor country. Amongst them are a dozen pregnant mothers-to-be and we are moving them to Samford. It will take about twelve hours for the round trip, so it's a big draw on us, the dogs, and our horses. Oh, and by the way, I was talking to the gardener earlier. He tells me that Ginger ripped into his prize plum tree.'

On that, as if on cue, Ginger let off the biggest fart I'd ever heard. Mr Lawler almost fell out of his saddle with laughter. I didn't say much. I was getting paid six shillings for tonight and I prayed that Ginger was up to it.

'Are we still good for four o'clock sir?'

'Yes we are. We have a pen number—lucky 13a. How about you and Ginger and Choc go to it and wait for me there?'

I knew once we left the sale yards there would be no turning back, world champion farting horse and all. However, I was not to know then that the term 'world champion' would play such an important role in my life.

Ginger was really starting to get into top gear, couldn't wait to get on the road. Mr Lawler and his support team arrived at the pen and we had a good chat about responsibilities. He explained that in order to gain the respect of the mob, I needed to walk my horse with purpose, keep it steady and never move faster than a walk. As he spoke, I couldn't help but feel pride once more. I was up on Ginger and Choc was walking beside me. All I could think was, *I am important I am working, I'm a useful person.* At that moment, I also realised that all the torment I copped at school seemed a lifetime away—but that's another story.

The terrible farting from Ginger had finally slowed up, for now anyway, and the best part was that we were walking into a light northerly breeze and I was at the at the back of the mob, if you get my drift ('drift' being the operative word). Before we knew it, we were well on the way heading along Lytton Road then Junction Road. We really didn't get a second look from the locals. Cars and trucks worked around us, and all went well. It all seemed normal; after all this was Cannon Hill, and this activity was a daily occurrence.

Moving up Morningside Hill, staying on the left verge of the road, the cattle were enjoying a green pick as they walked. A green pick is a strip of grass where the footpath meets the dirt road. I felt like telling them that the more they ate, and the quicker they ate, the shorter the time they would have in this world. But that is the life of cattle: they are born to be eaten. Tough words, I know, but it's the truth. In the years to come I would continue working in this environment, but I would never relax with the misery associated with a meatworks, and I carried those terrible thoughts and experiences with me until my end.

Strangely enough though, as we headed past the Morningside Cemetery, I had never thought much about human death. I had not had any relatives or friends die, so there was no reason to even connect my feelings about these poor animals to the human side of death. Yet here I was thinking about the cattle I was droving and realising that I would just have to put my sadness to one side if this was how I was going to make a living. I hoped that the rest would sort itself out.

While these thoughts were whirling through my head, I noticed a horse and cart coming towards us on the other side of the road. It was Mr Porter, the milkman. He now had a big strong Clydesdale which certainly looked the part. His son Des was alongside him. Des was in my class at Cannon Hill State School. I liked him and he liked me. We had both been bullied at school and both saw it as a normal occurrence.

Des and I were both in grade five. There were eight grades in our primary school, and the older kids in the higher grades took it upon themselves to beat and degrade the vulnerable kids in the lower grades. Things were that bad that I could not see my way past one more year. Mum knew the problem and Dad had been up to the school to see the headmaster, but he and Dad came to fisticuffs over the situation. To me, the headmaster was actually the root of the problem. He would walk around all day picking on all and sundry. I can still hear the sound of that bloody cane as he delivered six of the best. He actually prided himself on delivering the best possible strokes with the cane to inflict the most pain to the open hands of those that he decided needed straightening out. This cruel approach to holding order at the school—a sort of paradox within itself—only created mistrust and anger between the different ages of the kids at the school.

But for now, all of that was far from my thoughts and the least of my worries. *I'm not a school kid anymore, but a stockman, moving a hundred and ten head of cattle to a better place.* For a while, I even imagined that the owners would forget that they owned cattle grazing at Samford and would let these mothers have their calves and all live a long and happy life. It made me feel good to think that way. With all this daydreaming going on, I was surprised when I looked up and realised that we were now going past the Shafston Hotel where some of the local alcos and misfits had come out on to the footpath to cheer us on. I wondered if they thought I was important, maybe even Mr Lawler's son. Immediately I thought this though, I began to feel guilty. I shouldn't think like that. My dad had always been a good man to me, kind to Mum and sorry that he'd had to go to war. He rarely spoke about the war. It must have been hell.

Heading up towards the southern end of the Story Bridge, the mob were moving very well and I didn't have much to do other than look confident. Ginger was not farting nearly as much and Choc was on top of his game—his confidence was up and he was keeping one eye on me and one eye on the cattle. We were like a well-oiled machine.

At the end of Shafston Avenue I could see the Story Bridge which had not been long completed. The sheer size of the steel structure took my breath away. As we got closer, a strange-looking man with a large leather bag on his side waved to get our attention. Mr Lawler slowly walked Daniel over to the bag man whose job it was to collect the money for us to drive the cattle across the bridge.

'Good day Stan,' Mr Lawler said. 'How are you?'

'Not bad, no use complaining, no one listens anyway. How many head do you have?'

'Two stockman and a hundred and ten head.'

The fee was one penny per head for the cattle and threepence each for us.

The toll collector filled out the appropriate paperwork and then passed a docket to Mr Lawler which in time would be paid by the owners of the cattle. Once the transaction was completed, my new boss approached me, looking very serious.

'Okay, Roy', he explained, 'this is the tricky bit. Let's tighten them up so that there are no leaders. Once we are tight, keep Choc back. Light contact is the key.'

'I understand, sir,' I replied, trying to sound more confident than I felt.

As we moved across the southern end of the bridge, we were not under any of the steel structure, so the view to the east was magnificent. There was a ship in the Evans Deakin Shipyard. She looked like she was almost complete, ready to be launched. I wondered who she was for, and which oceans she would travel. To my left, I saw the dome of Customs House, the headquarters of the river, and two cargo ships being unloaded by hand by the wharfies. Dad had worked there from time to time. He actually liked it. Moving under the structure, I was thinking, *How the hell did all these pieces get into position?* Little did I know that three men had died during construction, falling to their deaths into the river below.

We were nearing the end of the bridge where there was a broken-down Queensland Brewing truck revving its guts out. Not surprisingly, this sudden noise was making the cattle edgy. You could sense that something was going to turn things arse-up. Mr Lawler responded quickly, cantering forward to stop the chances of a stampede, careful to keep Mitch and Gracey on his left so as not to spook the cattle. He headed them off without any fuss; a couple of quick cracks of his whip and me at the rear, gently slapping my hat on my thigh. The tension came out of the mob and on we went. I got a bit of a wave from the boss for the job I'd done of holding the rear and not letting the mob double back. The whistle my brother Harold had taught me came in handy for this line of work.

Soon we were heading along Gympie Road, coming through Kedron. Our target for water was Strathpine, a good spot to get off, have our sangers, and keep control of our mob while they took on water. The expectant cows seemed to be travelling well, even though a few of them were quite heavy in calf and teated up.

Our next stop would be Samford, so I was pleased to hear the call from Mr Lawler: 'All aboard!' I gathered the last of the mob from the shallow water and made sure that Choc was right by my side. Another crust of my sandwich did the trick. He was a solid dog. *He will be good around home,* I thought to myself. Of course, we'd had dogs before, but Dad had to put the last one down. For some unknown reason, he became savage and couldn't be trusted. Dad was very sad at having to do that. His years spent fighting in the war made him quite philosophical about the death of anything before its time. *He will welcome Choc in I am sure, and Choc will have as good a life as possible.*

Three and a half hours after leaving the watering hole, we still had about an hour to go until Samford. There were not many houses this far out of town, just small farms that provided fresh produce for the Brisbane fruit and vegetable markets which were held every Thursday morning. All of the fruit and vegetable shops in the area relied upon these market gardens for a reliable supply of fresh produce, in the same way as the local butcher shops did for fresh meat.

After such a long journey, Ginger was starting to get a bit sleepy, but I knew that we couldn't fall short now. I moved off the mob a bit and stepped Ginger up for a short sharp trot-canter in an effort to wake her up. She responded well. Back on the job. Just then, Mr Lawler gave me a shout and said that we were only a short distance from the Samford holding yards. As he said that, a rider on horseback came up beside me.

'Who is in charge, son?'

'Mr Bill Lawler.'

'Oh good, he knows what to do. Hey Bill, I'll go ahead and open the gate,' he called. 'Just keep them coming.'

'Okay, Rusty.'

Everything was going well, but as we pushed the last couple of head into the yard, I could see that one of the cows was prolapsing with calf. Mr Lawler saw her too and called to me, 'You better stay with her, Roy. The way she is going, the calf will be on the ground sooner than later.' Sure enough, a couple of minutes later, there it was. I got down from Ginger, pushed the other cattle away a bit, and knelt down. As I cleared the membrane away from its nostrils, the calf took its first breath. I had been involved in several calvings previously as we had a milking cow back home and Dad always kept her in full swing with calves. But I always thought that each birth was like opening presents: you never knew what you were going to get: boy or a girl, or maybe twins. That sometimes happened, but never to me yet. This time it was a girl—a Hereford cross breed, beautiful chocolate brown, and with one white rear foot. She was struggling to stand up, so I gave her a bit of a hand.

'Roy, let's move them through and sort out the other mums to be. No, on second thoughts, Rusty and I will do that. You hold the calf.'

'Okay sir.'

I was happy to stay back while the other men were put to the task of separating calving mums from the rest of the mob. But as I watched the newborn calf and its mother interact, I realised that something was wrong—the mother cow was pushing the newborn away when it tried to get to her udders to take on milk. I knew this could be a problem and so I called Mr Lawler over. He had finished sorting the herd and was soon back by my side.

'The little one is still trying to get to the business end of its mum to get some milk,' I explained, 'but the mum is still refusing to let the calf near her.'

Mr Lawler nodded and immediately tried an old stockman's trick of wiping the nose of the calf onto the nose of the mother, but to no avail.

'What do you think, Mr Lawler?'

'Well Roy, the mum is resisting the little one because she is exhausted and in such poor condition that she knows that she won't survive the situation herself. So nature guides her in how to survive and produce more calves when seasons get better. In regard to more feed being available, the calf's only chance of surviving is to find another mum or she will starve to death.'

I was heartbroken for the little one. 'Sir, can I take the calf back tonight on Ginger?'

'Lad, I know that you are upset by this, but to attempt to carry a calf on Ginger all the way back to Cannon Hill is a big call. Remember Choc has not had much to eat and Ginger has been at it for about seven hours.'

'I still have half of a sandwich I can give to Choc,' I responded immediately. 'That will give him a starter, and Ginger has not stopped eating at whatever patches of grass she can get her teeth into at every chance she gets, and there is plenty of water in the trough over there.'

'Yes, Roy, I know all that, but what about the calf? That little one needs milk now.'

Rusty, the other stockman, had now joined us and was in on the conversation. He was quick to point out that he was off on another mustering job and would not be able to back up with the special care that the calf would need. However, he said he had a starter bottle and teat for such situations and offered them to us. 'We can tie the mother short, get some milk from her and hand-feed the calf, ready for Roy and Ginger to walk her back tonight. We can even get a bit of extra milk for Roy's dog.'

I was so excited with the positive response from Rusty that I had forgotten who was in charge here. Of course it was Mr Lawler's call and he must have the last say. After all, if something went wrong, it was his reputation at stake, not mine or Rusty's.

'Well Roy?'

'Yes, sir.'

'I am going to go over the camp shed over there and make us both a cup of tea. Let's give it a try. It will certainly put our schedule back a bit but I am sure that your mum and dad will be glad to have another future cow in their midst.'

'Thank you, sir. I will give it my all.'

'I know you will, Roy, and I will be right behind you.'

'Thanks, sir,' I replied. A certain closeness came over the two of us at that moment, and I felt sure would last for the rest of my life.

While Mr Lawler was making us tea, I tied the cow to a rail of the cattle yard and used my hat to put milk into. It worked well because my hat was made from felt that came from rabbit skin. Next, I shaped my hat so that I could pour the milk into the bottle that Rusty had kindly lent us. The milk was not like our cow's at home; it was quite light in colour. *Oh well, better than nothing.*

The calf was not leaving her mum's side and it was surprisingly easy to convince her to take the teat of the bottle. She downed it happily, and her tail was wagging ten to the dozen as she finished off the bottle. After that, I milked the mother again to fill the bottle for the trip back to Cannon Hill. I shut the gate and left the mum and Soxy say their goodbyes. I'd called the calf Soxy because of her white foot.

All good. *I am important. I am producing for my family. It makes me feel good.*

'Boy, this cup of tea is a lifesaver.' (Another word that would come into my life down the track.)

'Yes, Roy, it certainly gives you a lift. We'll share the responsibilities of our horses carrying the little one back.'

'Thank you, sir.'

I now knew that with Mr Lawler's help in assisting with the rescue of Soxy, a positive result was a real chance.

'Well come on, Roy. I know that you are keen to get the calf back home, so let's do this. Grab a couple of those old hessian bags from over in the corner. We'll roll each of them up to put behind the pommel of our saddles.' The hessian bags padded the pommel and would provide some comfort to the calf over next five or six hours.

Ginger and Daniel were doing their best to eat as much quality signal grass as possible. I think the way they both looked at us was saying, *Please don't bother us now, we have some serious grass to eat. Letting you two fellas up on our backs at this time of night is unthinkable ... oh well you are the bosses.* With a bit of gentle persuasion, we managed to walk them away from their midnight meal. We walked over to the gate where the calf and mother were quietly standing and grabbed the calf.

'Roy, I'll untie the mother once you have taken the calf through the gate.'

'Okay, sir.'

'I have her and the calf is quite calm. I'll hold the calf while you mount Ginger.'

'Okay, pass her up, sir.'

She was resting across my lap on the hessian bags, and the three dogs were now up and on the job. They'd had a little sleep while all of the preparations were going on for our return home.

'Okay, we're on our way.'

As Rusty said his goodbyes, he took off his stockman's hat and gave his brow a wipe with his handkerchief, revealing the brightest head of red hair, which I am sure was the reason for his name. I had a bit of a chuckle to myself, as he put his hat back on and left us. You could sense his urgency to get home and into bed to be fresh for his next droving job. As he left us he called out, 'Let me know how Soxy goes the next time you see me, Bill.'

'Yes I will,' Mr Lawley said.

'Okay, Roy, you do the first shift; one hour each at a time.'

He pulled out his fob watch. It was almost one o'clock in the morning.

'How does it feel, comfortable?'

'Yes, very good.' I gave Soxy as much head comfort as I could. After all, she was only a few hours old. I wondered what was going through her mind as we walked away from the yards.

The dogs had taken up position; I realised at that moment that Choc was an excellent boy, and hoped that we would be together for a long time. I thought of Ginger too at that moment and hoped that she wouldn't get too tired. I was determined to get Soxy home. Although she probably weighed about fifty pounds, I was determined to not miss this opportunity of bringing home a great asset to my family. I suddenly realised that I had lots to be grateful for and my sense of pride swelled. I owned a horse, a dog, and a calf: *I am important, I have responsibilities, and I have a great family to go home to thanks to the efforts of my mum and dad.*

As we walked through the night, my thoughts soon turned to Mum, and I hoped that she would be proud of me. Even though Dad had been a great father, my feelings for Mum were eternal. I couldn't explain them. Mum was always there when I was sick, including after eating Mr Johnson's half-ripened peaches that Harold and I had pinched from the tree next door. It wasn't just that the peaches were green. We had jumped the fence in the dark, filled the bucket with as many peaches as we could, jumped back over the fence, and decided that we would eat some of the peaches in the dark before we went to bed. They tasted pretty good. It wasn't until we started vomiting that Mum had told us the peaches were all full of worms! We must have eaten six or so peaches each, and boy were we sick? I can still hear Mum telling us that we would both be okay once we got rid of all the worms that we had eaten in the dark. You know, from that day forward, I never took a second look at Mr Johnson's peach tree. A lesson well learned. Mr Johnson thought it was amusing when the word got out about our peaches heist, and just one wonderful Mum-story. *I love you Mum.*

We were moving along very well, and Mr Lawler and I had each had a turn at carrying Soxy, but I was back at my second hour and boy, was I tired. *Keep going,* I kept saying to myself, *it will be all over sooner than later.*

Mr Lawler estimated that after the next water break, we would still have two and a half hours to go before we were back in Cannon Hill, home. I thought I would sleep for a week when we finally got home, but I knew that I was responsible for Soxy so called out to Mr Lawler, 'I will do the last carry shift, sir.'

'No problem, Roy,' he called back.

Finally we were back walking down Morningside Hill, half an hour away from home. It was six thirty in the morning and pretty quiet really. We had to make just one more right turn and we would be back in Muir Street and up to our gate. I called out to Mum to come and see what I had brought home—not only a newborn calf, but a new dog, Choc. Well, she hurried down the front steps and I dismounted from Ginger. I was pretty well stuffed, and Choc was happy to lie down where he stood. When Mum gave me a big hug, I couldn't get the words out quick enough: a new calf and a new watch dog and of course six shillings. Mum thanked Mr Lawler for trusting me with such an important job. He tipped his hat and he, Daniel, Mitch and Gracey continued on up Muir Street into the morning gloom.

'I'm proud of you, Roy,' she whispered into my ear.

Dad was also quick to come out from under the house. He was in his beekeeping outfit as he had been robbing his bee hives early in the morning. He was a sight to behold! Bees terrified me. I'd had an incident once while helping Dad rob his hives; got stung from backside to breakfast time, not good. That is another Mum-story. She was there when it counted, nursed me back from the dead after all those stings. Dad said all I had to do was take a few early stings and the bees would have not got angry. But I was running around and around the backyard like my backside was on fire, until I nearly hung myself on the wire clothes line that stretched across our backyard. I hit the ground, and the swarm of bees that was chasing me suddenly caught up to me. Well, all hell broke loose. The bees got me good.

Dad went back under the house and got back into his normal clothes. He brought half a bucket of fresh milk for both Choc and Soxy from an earlier milking of our house cow, Jessey the jersey cow. I unsaddled Ginger and let her out of the front gate. The paddocks across the road had no fences, but Ginger never strayed. We were a team. Choc had some milk and Mum had a mutton bone she had been saving for a dog up the road.

'You feed her, Roy. She is your dog.'

By this time all of my brothers and sister had joined us. To my surprise, they were very excited about my adventure and kept asking all sorts of questions about my trip. I was bursting with happiness and my final thoughts before I collapsed with exhaustion were: *I am important, I am a stockman, I have a great family behind me, and most of all, my mum Minnie is proud of me.*

Chapter 2
Big Decisions

Before too long the holidays were over and it was time to head back to school. After the excitement of working and earning real money, I was definitely not interested in going back to school—especially as I suspected that things would be just as bad as before. I couldn't shake the feeling that all it gave me was misery and that every day was the same old thing. I felt like I wasn't learning anything, mainly because I was too scared to ask questions. Why couldn't I just keep working for Mr Lawler, or else go to the gate at Redbank Abattoirs and get a boy's job?

I had gotten nowhere with Mum and Dad who were not happy at all with the idea of me leaving school at such a young age, believing that an education was important. But to me, they seemed oblivious to the fact that being constantly picked on at school was destroying me. All of my brothers and my sister had left school at a young age, so why not me?

I went over to Mr Lawler's place to talk to him, hoping that he would support me, but Mr Lawler wanted no part in me leaving school either. 'I am sorry, Roy,' he said, 'I can't support you this time. I regret not having an education, and I want the best for you. Don't let the big schoolkids get to you. I'll talk to Tommy Holmes, the boxing trainer. See if he will teach you to fight, to sort out the bullies.'

'But, Mr Lawler…' I said.

'No, Roy, I mean it. You are not going to let these boys push you around.'

A couple of days later, I was standing in a boxing ring under Tommy Holmes' house. Mr Holmes was a short, wiry man, middle-aged with a pug nose from the odd round or two for a pound or two, and he was super fit. He showed me the basics: stance, defence, jab jab straight right; don't try to knock him out; just keep jabbing straight right. 'If you just throw medium punches, you will be able to keep your balance and land more punches. Keep those gloves up, never throw the first punch, let him throw a couple, and you defend. He will not expect that. Stand off him, let him get a bit tired, then pick him off, one barrage of jab jab straight right at a time. If you keep your cool, he will get the shits and try to heavy hit you. But you are too smart for him. Before he realises it, he is out of breath. Don't wrestle him; push him off. Jab jab straight right, okay? How often do you want to come?'

'Well, I can come Mondays, Wednesdays and Fridays. Will that do?'

'Yes,' said Mr Holmes. 'Every other day, I want you to do push-ups and sit-ups. I'll show you how: keep your body tight and put your nose to the floor for each push-up. I want you to do one hundred push-ups a day every day and the same in sit-ups.'

'Got it.'

'I will know if you are being fair dinkum or not. Mr Lawler has told me about what's going on at school. I can't guarantee that I can fix that but, if you follow my instructions, I do guarantee that after a few stoushes with a bully or two, the word will get out that you can go a round or two, and that will hopefully slow up the torment and give you some confidence. You are a naturally fit lad. I will see you Wednesday, four o'clock.'

Mr Holmes lived at Hawthorne, about a half an hour's ride away on Ginger. If nothing else, I knew I would enjoy the time with Ginger and, of course, Choc, my dog, who had settled into home life very well. Dad and Choc had bonded and were great mates. Choc now knew where he belonged, here at Muir Street.

I had eventually agreed to go back to school and keep my head down and try to stay out of trouble. 'Stay strong,' Dad would say. 'You have a plan.' So I started my workouts under the house.

My brother, Tom, was working at Redbank Abattoirs making tripe. I had not been to the meatworks yet as I was too young. You had to be twelve to get a job, so I resolved I might as well tough it out at school to the end of this year, grade six. Harold, my next youngest brother, was also keen to learn to fight, so at my next training session, I asked Mr Holmes if Harold could come as well.

'Yes, that will be fine,' he said. 'Tell him to start his exercises as well and come next Monday.'

'Okay I will.'

Meanwhile, I was jumping all over the place, trying to develop some boxing skills. It's okay to talk about it, but when you are standing in front of a boy nearly twice your size, and he is trying to knock your head off your shoulders, you start to learn really fast how to defend. Finally, after my fourth week, I was starting to get my act together—jab jab straight right, and keep moving.

Harold was starting to pick things up a bit too. He worked as a journeyman carpenter and he would catch a tram to training. Ginger, being at her prime, would double us up without a saddle on the way home. This was quite a skill, and after a few trips and a few fall offs, we were really enjoying ourselves—as brothers should.

Our little secret, though, was about to come to light. One afternoon after training, about four months into our training program, a couple of smart arses from school jumped out in front of Ginger. She swerved to miss them, and Harold came a cropper, falling off. I jumped off Ginger and got to Harold to see if he was okay. He was pretty mad, and he jumped up and started dancing around in front of the bigger boy who threw a punch or two but didn't connect. I looked at the other boy, and immediately I shaped up to him. Before we knew it, Harold and I were standing back to back, defending and jabbing. I took a couple of glancing hits to the right side of my head, but they didn't stop me from focusing on getting into top gear with my defending and jabbing. I didn't have to throw many rights as my left jabs to the head were doing the job. I didn't know how Harold was going, but I could hear him going for it. I could however hear some sobbing going on from his opposition so I knew he must have been really giving it to him.

'Go, Harold!' I yelled out, and a short time later all was quiet behind me. My opponent still wanted to go on with it, but I stepped forward, triple jabbed left and let go the best straight right of my career, followed by another. It was too much for him, and his large frame sank to its knees.

'I've had enough!' he yelled.

I hadn't realised how old these boys were. Much to our surprise, they got up and said nothing; they just walked away, heads down with shame. Harold and I knew that this was our biggest win so far, but were also smart enough to realise that it might also turn into our biggest loss. We knew that these two had plenty of mates and would be out to get square if the opportunity arose. And of course, I had to go to school tomorrow; that would be interesting. Without Harold, I knew I would be vulnerable.

We both decided that the only way we were going to stay on top was to bring in the big guns in the form of our next oldest brother, Tom. He was already known for his savagery as a street fighter. Maybe he would be willing to come to training and learn the trade of boxing? We spoke to him that night after a tense day at school, where I'd had a few glances from the enemy, from older boys, but to this point, nothing untoward had happened. Finally, Tom agreed to come to training and we were excited that he would give us a big advantage. If you want to launch big ships, you have got to find deep water. Tom was our deep water. His victories at the local School of the Arts dances were legendary.

It was never my intention to start a war in our neighbourhood, but a line had to be drawn in the sand between right and wrong, and with Tom's reputation and firepower, we as a family had achieved that. Don't step over that line unless you have carefully thought things through. Mum was a bit unsure of what was going on outside the boundaries of our home at Muir Street, but she trusted Tom's judgement of being fair and reasonable. The rest would sort itself out. Yorkshiremen are a proud lot and won't be compromised. Hundreds of years of survival have proven that.

Life for the next few months was calm. The boxing was ramping up to higher levels, and I was keen to move up, but my brothers were not as keen. I think in Tom's case, the rules of boxing were a bit restrictive; he was more of a street fighter. Sort of no holds barred. He could not see the sense of standing in front of someone and getting hit a few times. Why not just get hold of your opponent once you had identified him and at any cost beat him into submission? Don't give a mug an even break attitude. Far simpler, and you didn't need to train three times a week. It was a natural talent developed by hardcore experience from brawl to brawl. Rarely did he have to take a backward step. Harrold, on the other hand, was a softer person. Fighting in a ring was not his go either. He was always there when it counted, but the boxing in the ring was not for him. But I was still as keen as ever. I had been fighting at the Holmes gym for nine months and I'd had three in-house three-rounders with other training partners, and I must say that two wins and a draw was where I was at.

In spite of this success, my boxing skills were of no use at all when everything turned bad at school for the last time. The headmaster called me in and said that he had heard of the stance I'd made against older kids a few weeks before. He lined me up and gave me six of the best for—as he put it—'bullying' and for using my older brothers to stand over other boys in the higher grades. These were all delivered on one hand so that hurt a lot, but the worst thing was that he carried out the sentence on parade in front of the whole school, including the bullies. I tried my best not to cry, but the pain and humiliation were so bad that I could not help but get emotional. Of course, after that I was finished at school and I would carry being publicly beaten as a handicap for the rest of my life.

Dad was enraged, and the next morning was up going toe to toe with the headmaster again. This time, Dad had so much anger that he flattened the headmaster, accidentally grinding the brute's right hand into the concrete with his size eleven leather work boot. Of course, Dad was quick to point out that the headmaster was the instigator of the violence. Dad said, 'He won't be delivering any more six of the best for some time to come, if ever.'

Well done, Dad.

It took the family several days to settle however, especially after the local sergeant of Morningside police turned up to get Dad's side of the story. The old sergeant had been called to many homes for the same reason. There were no charges laid, and Dad settled down a week or so later. All Mum could do was bathe my hand. The blisters had broken and would take some time to heal. She was heartbroken by the actions of one man set to rule as he pleased with no accountability and no understanding of the damage caused by a public flogging in front of all of my friends; never would I forget it.

So, I was twelve years old and off to work, hardly able to scratch out my name. It seemed impossible that six years of state education had led to this. How could the education system be in such bad health? Remarkably, I was in the top half of the students in my class. Maybe things were so bad within the structure that the only way for the teachers to get through their bit was to have total control with the cane. I had heard of cases where young girls had been caned—unthinkable.

The rest of my family were supportive of my situation. We were a tight family, and it helped me get on with it. Choc knew that things had been a bit tense around the house, and he also was there whenever I needed just to sit and think. There was no rush. Dad was in full work, and his honey sales were up. I gave him a hand with the hives. It was hot, hard work. To give me more confidence with working with the bees, Dad bought me a full kit of beekeeper's clothes. I still had bad memories of the bees catching up with me in the backyard.

Life was getting back to normal. I owned a horse, a dog, and a calf that was growing up beautifully; she was eating grass now and stayed around the house. It wouldn't be long before she would be put to Mr Carlson's young bull, who, we noticed, was eager to get at her. But Christmas was only a stone's throw away and I had only saved a little from my odd jobs so I started to go down to the American army camp to try to earn some more.

About two thousand American soldiers had set up in camps along Tingalpa Creek, not far from home. They were waiting their turn to go and fight in the Pacific. They trained hard every day with their respective drill sergeants, who seemed quite extreme in their approach to the training program. Mr Lawler gave me the name of the soldier at the gate who would make up a list of names with their selection of groceries, cigarettes, no alcohol of course. The money was given to me to buy the essentials, and I usually got to keep the change, which was sometimes quite generous. However, sometimes the amount given was not enough to pay for that particular list of items. I didn't say anything though, as I was embarrassed with regard to my spelling and adding up the amounts. Somehow I got through it all and most days I left the camp with more money than I had gone there with. So with Christmas ten days away, I thought I would go into town and buy Mum a present.

Mum was a keen possum carer and looked after any young ringtail possums that were orphaned or injured and came her way. Mum would wander around the outskirts of our neighbourhood and cut off new gum tree shoots which were a delicacy for possums. Mum also gave some to Dad to develop his whistling prowess. When you split the gum leaf, a film of clear gum membrane exposes itself. This membrane is so fine that it produces a high whistle sound that, with a bit of tongue shaping, can be adapted to a sound like a harmonica. Dad and I became very good at it.

Mum didn't have a proper bush hat and scarf to go into the bush, so I decided to buy her a beautiful hat. Off I went, borrowing Harold's bicycle to get me to the tram terminus at Bulimba. The tram would take me into Queen Street in the city, where there was a shop that sold hats. I knew exactly what she needed, so I wouldn't settle for anything less. I had her size in inches, so was sure that all would be well. I jumped on to the tram at Bulimba and it took about forty-five minutes to get into Queen Street. The steel-wheeled tram was powered by electricity and directed via metal arms that connected with an electric cable suspended directly above the centre of the tram. Two people were in charge of the tram. The driver operated the throttle and brakes. Of course, no steering was required as the steel rails embedded in the road would take the tram to a terminus destination. The other person was the ticket person; this was a job for males and females.

It was raining, and the side curtains on the tram were lowered as we came over the Victoria Street Bridge, the entrance to Queen Street. A big department store, Coles, was my target for purchasing Mum's hat. When I entered the main front door, a large, strong-looking woman stood at the door checking all customers as they left the store for unpaid items. Her appearance was everything you would expect from a woman in that job. I thought of the list that the store manager would have drafted when he put the ad in the newspaper for positions vacant: wanted, strong, agile, fearless, emotionless, and able to defend herself if possible, and above all else, show no compassion. Yep, that would be the wish list for any store manager trying to defend his goods and his own job.

I made my way to the millinery section where there were dozens of ladies' hats to choose from. I was feeling a little embarrassed waiting for assistance. Maybe the attendant thought I was just a tyre-kicker, and I would move on. But I was here to buy a hat for Mum, and that was certain. Finally, a young lady asked me if she could help.

'Yes,' I said. My eye caught sight of a beautiful hat with a scarf. I checked the sizes, and there we were. I loved it. It was a dome-shaped safari hat with a three-inch brim and a light brown silk scarf to help keep the flies off when she was walking in the bush. Luckily, it was also in the Christmas sale at five shillings and sixpence. I still had twelve shillings left.

'Can you Christmas wrap it, please?' I asked the assistant.

'Yes, of course. Anything else?'

'Could you tell me where the men's shaving section is?'

'Down this aisle, to the end, and turn right at the end.'

I was getting Dad a new shaving brush because his old one was a military brush from the war with hardly a hair left on it. I chose a basic horsehair bristle for one shilling and threepence. I still had plenty of money left and would make even more when I got back to the army base in the morning. I was feeling pretty pleased with myself when I jumped on the next tram and back to Bulimba. All I could think about was Mum on Christmas morning.

When I got home, all was quiet. Mum was cooking fish and chips—it was Friday. Harold had been shooting mullet over at Tingalpa Creek and this was where the fish had come from. He had borrowed a service rifle from a friendly Yank, as Dad called them. Sometimes a couple of additional soldiers would come down to the creek, and they would place bets on who would shoot the biggest mullet. Before you knew it, a half dozen or so fish would be swimming around the surface with half their heads blown off. I would tell them to hold fire while I jumped in and threw the catch up on the bank.

Harold said, 'Thanks, boys, my mum will be grateful.'

While he was there, some of the soldiers asked if I was coming the next day. They said that they needed to order up big as they were shipping out soon. They would need plenty of cigarettes to get them through. 'Where are you going to fight: in New Guinea?' asked Harold, before wishing them luck and telling them to 'stick it up those Japs' arses.'

'We will give all we have, Harold,' they replied, adding that it had been good knowing us Holland boys.

Mum was an expert fish filleter and took little time to have the twelve fillets of mullet battered and ready to go into the pan of dripping. She cooked on a wood stove, and as December was our hottest month, the kitchen was as hot as Hades. Mum always precooked the potato chips in the pressure cooker so that they didn't need too much frying. The dripping made the fish very crisp.

'Best fish and chips ever,' I always said.

I always hung close to Mum's sleeve to get any small crispy bits that happened to fall my way; thanks, Mum.

I would sometimes say to her, 'What's for tea, Mum?'

She would say, 'Pig's bum and bickies, son.'

I would say, 'I bags the bickies, Mum.'

It was a line that we both worked for the crowd; the only thing missing was the crowd. Well, that's show business. It didn't matter. I was with Mum, and that was all that mattered.

On December twenty-third, just before Christmas, Dad told us that something very special was going to happen at four o'clock that afternoon. He said that he would need all of us boys to give him a hand to move something upstairs. We were all in the kitchen chattering and waiting while Mum was plucking feathers from two roosters that Dad had given the chop earlier in the day. Dad had picked a pumpkin and dug fresh potatoes for Christmas lunch as well.

A truck horn sounded, and we all went out to see who it was and saw a truck parked out the front of our house. Two strong-looking men were lowering the tailgate. Dad was first to be down the stairs to open the double gates. None of us were any the wiser until the truck drivers were man-handling a cream coloured box. By this time, Mum had also come to the front landing. She was first to call out, 'John, what have you been up to?'

'It's okay, Minnie; I will have it paid off in no time.'

Well, it was out of the truck, standing on the ground, waiting for us boys to get our brand new electric Kelvinator refrigerator into the house.

Ernie was first to work out how to open the door, but Dad was in a hurry and called, 'Now come on, boys, let's not fuss around. Let's get it up those stairs and into the kitchen.'

The four of us got around the fridge and Dad said, 'On the count of three ...' Of course, someone had to direct the traffic. We were at the bottom step of fourteen. I used to count them every day I came home. Ernie and I were at the top of the fridge, and Harold and Tom had the heavy end. Tom was a very strong and fit man, so it was natural that he would take the brunt of the quite heavy fridge. One step at a time, and we were at the top. The kitchen was at the back of the house, so all the way through the house we went. By this point, Mum was throwing the weight of her tiny frame around, directing and giving advice on how to lift and walk at the same time. It must be a woman thing. She had to have the last word, and Dad was beaming with pride. Rita was backing Mum up, of course, working out where it would go. Well, that was obvious; there was only one power outlet in the kitchen, and that was beside the sink. Perfect.

By now, the two delivery men had made it into the kitchen had not needed to lift a finger. Nobody cared.

'I will show you how it works,' said the man in charge. 'You plug this cord into this socket and set the temperature on this dial to cold and turn it on.' As he did, all the lights went out. Well, Dad was first to go off the handle. None of us moved; we just looked quizzically at the man in charge, who kept his composure and said to Dad, 'Where is the fuse box?'

Dad said, 'Follow me.'

Under the house was a wooden box that had been installed by both an electrician and the power company when the builders had built the house. The delivery man slid back the small door at the back of the box as all hell broke loose. When the door opened, a couple of Mum's ringtail possums jumped out of the box. One landed on top of our expert's bald head and in its panic to get away, scratched his head. Blood started to run down his face.

Wow, what's next?

He pulled out his handkerchief and cleaned himself up a bit to try and get some composure. To take control of the situation, and that was to install a refrigerator, he pulled a small roll of wire out of his top pocket, explaining that he needed to install heavier fuse wire into the fuse that was going to run the fridge. A pair of pliers and a screwdriver did the trick. He turned the main power switch back on and went back to the kitchen where, voila, the Kelvinator was humming away.

Dad was not convinced and demanded that the two delivery men stay until the fridge showed some sign of getting cold. They explained how the freezer worked and filled the ice tray up with water to show us how now we could make ice blocks overnight. Wow! By this time, the inside of the fridge was actually starting to get cold.

'Amazing,' was all Mum could get out.

'Shut the bloody door, Minnie.'

'Just sign here, Mr Holland.'

Little did Dad know he would still be paying it off for years to come. Welcome to hire purchase. 'The bees will be working overtime from now on,' Dad said as he signed his life away.

The fridge cost Dad fifty pounds ten shillings; he only had to pay five quid up front. The way Dad looked at it, if we all had to kick in down the track, we would as a family, but for now, nothing should spoil the merry Christmas moment for Minnie.

The hard part now was to tell the iceman that we no longer needed ice.

'Leave that to me, Minnie.'

'Thanks, John. I will. The iceman is due this afternoon, and we pay as we go, so we don't owe him any money.'

'Good, that will make it easier, I guess.'

I remember that Dad said he was quite humbled by the iceman's response when told the news about our refrigerator. After all, for many years, this man had battled extreme heat, terrible storm conditions and extended our credit from time to time. To tell him that we no longer needed his service was more difficult than Dad had imagined, but he simply thanked the family for our custom and then congratulated Dad on his success in raising such a fine family.

'See you around, Stanley,' Dad said. It was probably the first time Dad had called Stanley by his full first name, as a sign of respect.

On Christmas morning I was up early in anticipation of a small present. I had put the hat I had bought for Mum under the tree and also Dad's shaving brush. I could see a small present with my name on it. *I must wait for Mum and Dad to get up before I can open it.*

My brothers and sister didn't buy presents for each other at this stage, as money was always tight.

I went and opened the fridge, and in the door were six bottles of beer, only small ones, and the two roosters were icy cold. Lunch would be good.

'Hello, Dad.'

'Merry Christmas, Roy.'

Mum put her head around the corner and said the same. She was wearing her dressing gown even though it was quite warm. I loved the Mum-smell of her dressing gown; so did the rest of us.

Soon, we were all up, and Mum was passing around each of our presents. I opened mine, and with delight, I found a new stockman's belt just like Mr Lawler's. It was handmade by Mr Lawler himself, who was a leather craftsman, and the belt would last a lifetime. Mum was trying on her hat and looked wonderful in it. She'd be able to wear it in the bush, as I had planned. Dad went out to the kitchen and had a shave.

I can't remember what everyone else got, but we were all very happy and looking forward to lunch. Mum had invited the old bloke from down the road because he had no family. He promised Mum that he'd have a bath before he came up to lunch, whether he needed to or not. I am pretty sure he would only tub on a couple of occasions a year.

'All creatures great and small,' Mum would say, 'creature' being the operative word for today anyway.

Mum and Rita did a great job with lunch. The only disappointed attendees were the two roosters: they weren't happy at all. Mr Jenkins, on the other hand, went over the top and down the other side in his efforts to impress us. He wore a suit, which was highly irregular. He also brought flowers for Mum. God knows whose front garden they had been stolen from on his way up the road! Dad made a comment after his arrival that he was probably doing a line for Mum. If Mum had heard that, she would have hit Dad over the head with one of the roosters. She didn't tolerate small talk, especially when she was the centre of the joke. I think Dad sort of regretted his statement, but I think the bottle of beer had loosened his tongue a bit. The beer at lunch was quite a treat and would become a ritual at all our future Christmases.

Pudding was the usual plum and custard, with a threepence hidden inside. I was a bit worried about where the plums had come from, but Dad assured me that he knew of a plum tree over in Hoges's paddock on Creek Road, beside an old abandoned slaughterhouse that had closed some twenty years ago. He said that the plums were so perfect that when you picked them and held them up to the sun, you could see your finger on the other side. I had my doubts, but put it to memory for down the track.

We had a family chat about the fridge and the repayments. Ernie, who was our eldest brother, said that he thought we should all contribute towards paying off the fridge. It was agreed that we each would put in five shillings a week. Ernie had looked at the repayments, and worked out that if we went along the path of hire purchase, we could have bought two fridges, not one. Ernie agreed to manage the gathering of the funds and depositing the money monthly at the post office.

All this time, I was thinking about my year to come. I couldn't rely on the army camp anymore as the Yanks were all being sent away to fight, so I would have to go and stand at the abattoir gates and wait for a boy's job. That was my best and only choice. At first I thought I would talk to Mum and Dad tomorrow, but changed my mind and decided to say it right now, in front of everybody.

Without warning, I suddenly stood up. 'Mum and Dad, I am going to go and get a boy's job at Redbank Abattoir, starting as early as next week,' I announced with more confidence than I felt.

There was complete silence, then Dad responded, 'Roy, we are disappointed that you have to do this, but Mum and I understand.'

'And you have our full support,' Tom chimed in, going on to say that he would get the name of someone in the know on the beef floor. This would mean maybe pushing gut barrows or something. I thanked him but said I preferred it if I could go and start at the bottom and work my way into a good position.

On that, Dad gave three cheers for Mum and Rita, and that was it. Our guest left, and most of the family went off for the traditional Holland snooze after lunch. Later, Dad and I agreed to spin a few honey frames together as he had a few orders to fill and he was keen for the money after Christmas.

Chapter 3
Uncharted Waters

1943 was a big year—I started work and I hung up my boxing gloves in favour of swimming. Little did I know that this new direction would change the art of swimming forever—not just here in Cannon Hill, but the world.

I had been going swimming at our school pool because we had a teacher that could swim and we had two lessons a week. I realised the lessons would all be over if I did not go back to school. I had picked swimming up quite quickly and gained enough confidence to go and swim at an old disused quarry that had filled up with water over the years. It had high cliffs on the eastern side, and the water was crystal clear. The quarry had been the source of shale rock, the perfect road base for our new streets of Brisbane. We did not have bitumen at this point, and the shale made a great durable surface for both horse and cart and motor vehicles alike. A steamroller would continually rotate its way through the area. First, a horse-drawn grader with a blade would smooth out the bumps as best it could, then the steamroller would slowly pass over the semi-levelled surface. The roller was powered by steam, generated by burning coal in a steam boiler. I loved it when the driver would pull the rope and make the machine whistle. In all of my days to come, I never heard a whistle that sang that note; I loved it.

The second big change was of course work. My first day was the third of January 1943. I woke up early and was going to ride my bike up to the meatworks gate and apply for a boy's job. It didn't matter what it was; I had committed to my family to pay five shillings per week until the fridge had been paid for. But before that, I needed a trip to the backyard outhouse. I was standing in line up the backyard at home, waiting for those who got up earlier to do their business, but unfortunately, I was fourth in line. Then Dad came along and of course he had priority so suddenly I was fifth. Dad was getting on a bit; he was now sixty-nine years old and his lungs were suffering from the gassing that he got in the war. So, although he was still working, he was given a bit of slack with the jobs he was allocated, in an effort to keep the Holland family financially afloat. After all, four boys and a girl was a great contribution to the rebuilding of Australia after the First World War

While you were queued up for the toilet, there was nothing much to do but wait for your brothers or sister to do their business. There was sometimes a bit of heckling, especially if one of us took a bit longer than normal, but what was normal? I think it was about three minutes. If it was raining, we were able to stand in a shed that Dad had built especially. It had no sides, just six posts and a corrugated iron roof, with an old sulky up the back. We weren't sure if the sulky would ever see the road again as things were moving forward with motor cars. In the same way that refrigerators were the future, cars were here for better or for worse.

Finally, on this my first day of work, it was my turn. I was worried though, as I knew that the dunny man was coming tomorrow, so that meant that the tin would be getting dangerously full. The dunny man's job was to bring a fresh tin and fresh sawdust that would be kept in an open box beside the dunny box. After you did your business, you would sprinkle a handful of sawdust over your droppings to keep the smell down. He would pull the full tin out, push the new tin under the drop zone, then put the lid on the full tin. He wore a padded flat hat, and as strange as it may seem, once he had a bit of swinging space, he would swing the full tin up into the air and put it on top of his head. Thus goes the saying 'as flat as a dunny man's hat'. They worked for Hunter Brothers and were a special breed of men. The thing I remember about them was that they were very business-like and they were spotless and surprisingly clean. I guess it would have been a long day at the office if things got out of hand with drizzle and spillage. They never stopped and said hello or any small talk. I guess it would've been hard to think of what you could say to a man standing in front of you with a tinful of shit on top of his head.

I could still hear the roar of the dunny man's truck. They always stayed in first gear to reduce the risk of having to stop suddenly and cause a real mess. They would jump fences sometimes, depending on the weight of the tin. The dunny man was just another unsung hero in the early days of suburbia.

Up the back stairs, Mum had made me some—you guessed it—corned beef and pickle sandwiches, along with toast and a couple of fried eggs with a cup of tea for breakkie. Once I had eaten this feast, I was off, wearing a blue singlet and matching blue work shorts that Harold gave me. I hoped that two sets of clothes would get me through, but little did I know what was coming in a couple of hours.

I borrowed Harold's bicycle for the ten-minute ride to the meatworks' gate. I had been past these gates many times when I was going fishing with Harold in the past, but didn't take notice of how well kept the rose gardens were down both sides of the entrance. There was a line-up of men at the gate, but I could only see one other boy, and I sort of recognised him.

Mum had written a short note allowing me to get a boy's job. When she handed it to, me there were tears in her eyes.

'Don't worry, Mum, all will be well.'

'I hope so, Roy.'

Finally, it was my turn to give my name to the man that handed out the jobs. I gave him the letter.

'Ah, Tom Holland's brother. Can you fight as well as he can?'

'Yes,' I said, 'I was taught by Tommy Holmes, the meat inspector.'

'Well, I am sure you have been taught properly. Mr Holmes has a good record, yes he does.'

'I would like to think that my fighting days were behind me,' I said.

I also didn't want the gateman to think that I was a show off.

'Have you got any experience here lad?'

'No, but I'm keen.'

The telephone rang a couple of times.

'Yes, I do have a couple of boys here … ah the boning room, yes I will send them both down right away. Names are Roy Holland and Billy Cummins … yes I have their details. I'll pass them on to the pay clerk and they can fill out their hours as they go.' He hung up the phone. 'Good news, boys, you start in the boning room. Follow the two railway lines to the end. The office is on the right. The foreman's name is Ferpo Neuman.'

'Okay.'

I grabbed my lunch bag, shook hands with Billy and we quickly walked together to the end of the tracks where a tall, dark-skinned man in a blue flannel shirt and long pants and boots was waiting. He looked us up and down and said that I would stay here at this level and Billy would be up on top of the boning tables. 'Your jobs are to keep the floors and boning tables clear of all the trimmed waste pieces of meat. Here is your broom, Roy, and Billy, you use this scraper. Roy, you push your bits and pieces into piles then push the piles toward that hole in the floor.'

'Okay, sir.'

'Don't call me sir; my name is Ferpo. Okay? And Bill, you work with a gut bucket up on that bench that the boners are working on. Your job is to keep things up there free of any offcuts. As you fill it, you also tip it down the hole.'

'Where does it all go, Ferpo?'

'Down to the digester.'

'What is that?'

'It is where a big steam barrel cooks all the offal with steam. The oil and fat that are left at the end is called tallow, and soap is made from it. All the shit that is left is pumped to the river.'

I was gob-smacked. *Soap comes from dead animals?* Billy was a bit quiet. *He'll be okay*, I thought.

'Let's go, boys. But work well. If you muck up, the boners will give you the drill.'

When we arrived, the men called boners were all going flat out. They had a bucket on their hips with a couple of knives in it and a sharpening steel hanging off their belt. They used the steel to keep touching up their knives as they went about their day. I didn't acknowledge anybody. I just started fumbling my way around, trying to pull all the waste bits from around the bare feet of the boners. I was also a bit quiet; this was not quite what I had in mind. *It's a job.* I kept thinking of the dunny man and I felt better.

I started to get some rhythm. I was covered in blood. You couldn't avoid the splashing of blood that went on when about twenty boners were doing their thing. They had a tally system like everybody else here. When the tally for the day was done as a group, they went home and got a full day's pay. No one wanted to be in this place any longer than you had to be. The smell of death never left you and you were surrounded by noisy clanging, singing and yelling.

The meat that had been deboned was heading for the giant freezer rooms at the end of the boning room. A cargo ship was tied up at the wharf; it had to be filled with deboned and half-carcasses of beef. Finally, a horn blew and all went quiet. I went up to the washstand to clean my body from my shoulders and down my arms before using a towel to dry myself off. Billy was just beside me and we grabbed our lunch bags and went down and sat on the wharf. Billy couldn't eat. He was just quiet. I left him alone and found I had no trouble hoeing into my smoko. Twenty minutes goes quickly when you don't have a watch. The horn went off again and we were back into it full bore.

The boners were a friendly lot, always taking the piss out of us boys, and by lunchtime, I was feeling better and more comfortable. Lunch was thirty minutes. Same deal, Billy was still quiet and it was hard to get 'boo' out of him. I just left him alone, deciding he would either get on with it or not turn up tomorrow.

The pace after lunch picked up even harder. A tough, tattooed young bloke was yelling out, 'Come on you bastards, go harder!' and harder they went. It was 1.30 in the arvo and I could see some of the workers at the other end of the boning room start walking forward toward the end where I was working. They joined in with the men at this end to finish off the tally together and the day for them was done. I still had a bit of sweeping to do. As I pushed the last pile down the hole in the floor, a man in a raincoat and gumboots came with a large fire hose, blasting his way from the other end to this end of the shed. He had obviously done this many times before. There were several grated drains that the floor sloped towards, and after he had done his bit, Billy and I cleaned out each of the grates, placing bits of fat and off cuts in to a couple of buckets and sending them down the hole in the floor. We were done also.

All of the boners had gone to the change rooms and showers beside of the boning room, but neither Billy nor I had a change of clothes so we showered in our work clothes and agreed to both bring fresh clothes tomorrow.

'Seven o'clock start. You okay, Billy?'

'Yes, I am just a bit nervous about the whole thing.'

'Yes, I know what you mean, but you know what, they are great blokes to work with.'

'Yes,' said Billy. 'They are good blokes.'

'Where did you go to school, Bill?'

'Morningside State School.'

'Any bullying?'

'Shit, yes, that is why I left.'

'Me too,' I said,

We were both dripping wet but it did not matter. I saw some of the boners dressed in their street clothes and noticed they were well dressed and looked like any other man in the street. I guess it was just like any other job: it was just a job, and you did what you had to do to get through.

On Harold's pushy on my way home at 2.15, it seemed that everybody was working on the tally system. The harder you worked the earlier you got to go home. By the time I got home, I was almost dry.

'Boy its hot, I think I'll go for a swim over at the quarry, Mum.' She was in the garden and Dad hadn't got home yet.

'How was it, Roy?'

'It was good, Mum. I'm in the boning room with a Morningside boy called Billy Cummins.'

'Oh that is good. Are you working tomorrow?'

'Yes,' I said. 'There is a ship in and we have to fill it with beef. The boners say that it will take at least three weeks to fill it. The ship is called the *Belfast Star* and she is from Ireland. I wonder where that is.'

'Roy, it's a country near England.'

'Oh, thanks Mum. I am going to the quarry for a swim.'

'Don't be late.'

'What's for dinner?'

'Pig's bum and bickies, Roy.'

'I bags the bickies, Mum.'

Ten minutes later I was on the edge of the quarry. In I went. I wasn't much of a swimmer. I couldn't get the breathing bit, so I kept my head out of the water and kicked and stroked. It worked for me.

By now, it was just after three o'clock and a lot of my school mates were coming down for a swim.

'Hey Roy, where were you today?'

'I'm not coming back. I have a job at Redbank, as a boy.'

'You lucky bastard,' said Jonny Cash, a boy I had grown up with and a good friend. Out of the corner of my eye I saw a couple of the bullies that had been the cause of me leaving school.

'G'day you two pieces of shit!' I yelled out.

They were a bit startled by my comment and they knew that I was not scared of them at all. If anything, they had every reason to fear me. With the backup that my brother Tom had created, they didn't offer reprisal. They just swam to the other end of the lake. By this time, a couple of other kids had arrived, jumping in and dog paddling their way around.

As I floated around I thought to myself once again, *Life is good. I have a job, I earn money, I am helping the family buy a refrigerator, I have a great family, I have a horse and saddle a dog and a cow, well done.*

When I got home, Mum had cooked sausages, mash, and peas all from our garden except for the sausages which came from Feuerriegals' butchery down at the shops in Wynnum Road. Harold was explaining that he had met a man called Bill Flemming who was in charge of a freshwater pool at West End beside the Brisbane River. Mr Flemming held advanced swimming lessons there and Harold was going to go and learn how to swim better. Harold had made a new batch of friends where he worked and they were all good swimmers.

'I am going to start on weekends.'

'What time do you go on Saturday, Harold?'

'You'll have to catch the tram, Roy. I am going down to the surf club at Tugun.'

'Where is that, Harold?' Ernie chimed in.

'Well it is near Coolangatta. I have never been there, but the train leaves at 7.00 am Saturday morning from Roma Street Station and drops us off at the Tugun Station around lunchtime. The surf club is on the edge of Tugun beach.'

'Wow, can I come?' I asked.

'I'm sorry but you have to be able to swim 400 yards in under eight minutes. That is eight laps of the Valley Pool.'

'Where is the Valley Pool?'

'Don't worry about that yet. Start your training with Mr Flemming on Saturday. Tell him what your target is and he will get you there. You better hurry up because the surf season finishes for the year at the end of April.'

'Okay, I am on to it. how much does Mr Flemming charge?'

'Two bob each session. He corrects your style and gets you swimming.'

'I am swimming a lot better,' said Harold, 'and I'm starting to enjoy it.'

Mum and Dad just shook their heads. 'What next, our boys are going to swim in the ocean?'

Harold was quick to correct Mum. 'Swim in the surf.'

'What is that?'

'Waves, Mum.'

'Oh.'

We all got in and cleared the table and washed up. Dad always said that a family that washes up together stays together, and he was right. With the washing up done, Harold and I decide to call it a day. We shared the same bed and slept head to toe. Our house was only two bedroom so all sorts of areas were created to set up beds for the entire family.

'Good night, Harold.'

It seemed that my head had only just hit my pillow when Mum's alarm clock jumped into life, loud enough to wake up the neighbours. Five thirty am. I had intended to try and beat the alarm and be first in the dunny.

Bugger. Three in front, but that's not too bad. At least I am in front of Rita. She can take forever sometimes. Ah in I go; the tin is dangerously full and the dunny man will not be happy. He'll be here this morning. I don't want to be here when he sees the condition of the tin.

Mum knew how to handle him. She'd tell him he should have come earlier. Her family couldn't help it; they were all hardworking and ate a lot. He'd have to be on his toes when he put this one on his head. We all have a job to do.

'Thanks for breakkie, Mum.'

'I made you peanut paste sandwiches, for a change.

'Thanks. Remember I will buy my lunch from the canteen on Thursdays, Mum.'

I was off, peddling as fast as I could into the boning room ten minutes early. Some of the boners were sharpening their knives. Buster Peters was a master of his trade and he said that it was all about your knives.

'How sharp are they, Buster?'

He pulled a hair from his head and held it up to the light coming from the open door at the end of the room. The hair was vertical above his thumb and index finger. Then he put the sharp edge of the knife up to the hair and pushed the knife against the hair. Because hairs are hollow, the blade split the hair. A small curl of hair was left on the blade of the knife. Amazing.

'That's sharp,' Buster said. He said if you cut your finger, you didn't even feel it.

The horn went off and the noise cranked up. There seemed to be a bit of discontent amongst the men. I asked Buster what the problem was. Ferpo, our foreman, was up arguing with a couple of the men on the other side of the room. The cattle that they were breaking down were bigger than normal. I could see from where I was working that the carcasses were a lot bigger than usual. I kept my head down and arse up; not my problem.

Ferpo, was now using his skills to keep the pace going. He moved two other boners over to share the extra weight that had to be dealt with to get the meat off the bones of the bigger cattle. Things settled and away we went again, full bore.

The owner of the works, Mr O'Boyle, was on the floor. He appeared from nowhere, saying his hellos to Ferpo. He walked over to the two boners that were having a whinge. I must say that whatever was said between the two parties seemed to settle things completely. There was no misunderstanding of who was in charge of this place. Mr O'Boyle. I will remember that.

Ferpo walked my way with Mr O'Boyle and Ferpo introduced the boss to me. Although I had blood all over me, he still looked me in the eye, grabbed my hand, and gave me a firm shake.

'Welcome, Roy. I wish you well here. Handling it okay, are you?'

'Yes I am, sir.' And sir it was, and sir it will be.

'Good luck, son,' and they moved on, talking about progress and how the kill would have to increase next week to finish off the shipment going to England in a fortnight.

'We can handle it, sir,' Ferpo reassured his employer of twenty odd years.

'I know you will, Ferpo. That is why you're the top dog in this area.'

'Thank you again, Mr O'Boyle.'

On that, the men parted and I could tell Ferpo had an extra bounce in his step as he walked over to his office.

The horn blasted. Lunch. I was starving, so Billy and I went into the lunch room. I now even had a metal pannikin to drink my tea from.

I was getting into the rhythm of things in the boning room. The end of my third day was coming up, so lunch from the canteen tomorrow. That would give Mum a break from making lunches. She always said that she didn't mind, but five sets of sandwiches a day was a lot of sandwiches. *I love you Mum,* I thought. Mum was only a small woman but her size had nothing to do with the size of her heart. My cup runneth over.

The men were well into their lunch break when a man who I had not seen before stood and addressed the others. He introduced himself as

Jim Wilson, the new union delegate. He welcomed Billy and me into the clan, then asked if there were any grievances that were outstanding from the last monthly meeting. One of the boners stood up and explained that there should be better communication between management and us on the floor.

'What do you mean? I'm sorry I don't know your name as this is my first day here with you.'

'Bluey Philips is my name.'

'Thank you. So what do you mean?'

'Well today was a perfect example. Big cattle need more hands and we do fewer cattle, therefore the tally numbers should be reduced so that the knock off time after the tally can be reached in normal time. We're producing the same amount of cattle but we're producing a greater volume of boned meat; we deserve overtime to produce the extra boned meat.'

'I take your point, Bluey. What is the feeling of the rest of the meeting?'

There was a lot of over-talking and chatter. Then a man stood up and quietly asked for permission to speak. His name was George Johnson. George was a quietly-spoken man but spoke well.

'Please go ahead, George.'

'I think that the management do a bloody good job of keeping us in work pretty well all year round, year after year. I am grateful that Mr O'Boyle still keeps us on carrying out maintenance and elsewhat when it is tough and cattle numbers are down, so that we can still take home our weekly pay. I vote that we take the good with the bad.'

'Let's have a show of hands. All those in favour of continuing on with the current situation of small cattle, big cattle, a tally is a tally. All those in favour? And I must remind our two new boys that until they are financial they cannot cast their vote.'

'I understand,' I called out.

'Well all in favour, raise your hands.'

I saw no need for a count. Carried unanimously, even Bluey put his hand up, that was good. I thought at least we had addressed the issue. Jim Wilson closed the meeting and thanked the men for their input.

'I will see you next month, unless something unforeseen comes and you need support. Oh and you two new boys, I'll come and see you at smoko tomorrow.'

I gave him my nod, and then went back to work.

'First pay tomorrow, boys!' someone called out. I hadn't even thought of it. *Payday tomorrow, I wonder how much I will get. I hope it is more than five shillings for the fridge.*

The rest of the day went quickly. There was always plenty to do and the boners were very particular about a clean work area. Day three came to a halt, the hose man giving his hose every opportunity to get into every nook and cranny to wash out any chance of smell that would become unhealthy during the night. Redbank Meatworks had an impeccable record when it came to hygiene. The meat inspectors assigned to this area were always on the guard for any slip-ups in this matter.

Riding home was better, cooler. I could see a thunderstorm in the distance, moving towards my part of Brisbane. *I had better rush it; Ginger can get a bit uneasy in a thunderstorm I don't want her to bolt,* I thought to myself. *She could end in up in a barbed wire fence.* That often happened around our paddocks, but when I got home, there she was, standing at the gate of our house. When we made eye contact, Ginger gave a big head shake and settled. I opened the gate and walked her up to Dad's shed beside the dunny, and she willingly came in out of the rain that had now started to fall. I started to give her a brushing, which was much to her liking. She gave a whinny or two, enjoying a couple of handfuls of wheat and a couple of Dad's homegrown corn cobs. She was at home in the shade as the storm really cranked itself up into top gear. I hoped Dad's shed would hold up in the wind that was swirling around the backyard.

Fifteen minutes or so later, the afternoon sun was starting to break through to the west. Tom came up to use the dunny. 'Hi Roy, how was your day? Are you getting a fair go?'

'Yes, Ferpo is firm but fair.'

'All you can ask, Roy. I'll see you on the way back. Ginger's in good shape.'

'Thanks, Tom. She has a good life. I'm going to ride her into Balmoral train terminus and back on Saturday, before heading to Davies Park.'

'That will keep her sharp,' said Tom.

'Yes it will,' I replied.

On his way back to the house, Tom stopped and asked what I was doing at Davies Park on Saturday.

'I am going to learn how to swim, properly.'

'What is properly?'

'Well, I am about to find that out.'

Harold had been going several times a week for the last month or so. I'd watched him swim over at the quarry last week and he swam with his head in the water, then turned his head and took a breath. He was beginning to move faster in the water. Of course, he was showing off a bit, but that was okay.

'This Mr Flemming is a good man who only charges two shillings a lesson and it is for one hour,' I explained.

'I bet you will be stuffed after that, Roy.'

'By the way Tom, it's payday tomorrow. How much do you think I will get for four days' work?'

Tom responded and said with his tongue in his cheek, 'About fifty quid I reckon.'

'Fifty quid!' I excitedly replied.

Tom gave a loud laugh and said, 'No Roy, you will have to wait. I am not a pay clerk, so wait and see, and when you do open your pay packet, you will get the same rush that we all got when we opened our first pay packet. You will never forget it, I promise you. I am going up to peel some potatoes for Mum's corned beef and cabbage.'

'Great stuff,' I responded. 'Okay, Ginger, let's put you back in the paddock across the road for a couple of days until Saturday morning, when you'll earn your keep as we canter our way to Balmoral. We will see how fit you are, old girl.'

On my way back, I could see a couple of Mum's ringtail possums walking upside down along the electric wire that ran from a large timber pole to the side of our house. Somehow, they could get from the fuse box under the house up to the fascia board at the soffit, then walk upside down along the wire till they got to the pole. When it was dark enough, they would scurry down the pole and forage on Dad's and Mr Johnson's fruit all night. Early in the morning, under the cover of darkness, they would repeat the process in reverse, back into the safety of the fuse box.

We were one short for tea that night, because Ernie was taking a girl up to the Astra Picture Theatre. I wondered why Ernie would miss a serve of Mum's corned beef and a follow up of apple pie. Oh well, there must be a good picture show on for him to miss out on this.

'Hey, Mum, can we divvy up Ernie's portions, seeing that he is not here?'

'No, Roy. I'll be putting his in the oven for when he gets home. All that loving can make you hungry.'

Dad piped in with a comment. 'It might not just be food he is hungry for.'

'Now come on Dad, you have no right to go down that track. Ernie is a well-mannered young man and I am sure he'll do the right thing.'

'What is the right thing?' asked Rita.

'Well you know, do the right thing.'

'Oh,' I said, and left it at that.

Mum bundled up Ernie's portion of beef and of course apple pie, and put it in the oven that was now starting to cool down. Well, a bit of small talk, into the dishes and off to bed. Harold talked for a while about swimming and our next adventure, surf lifesaving. I said, 'Harold did you enjoy your apple pie tonight?'

Harold said he particularly liked Mum's crust.

'I don't know how she does it, but her crust is the business, don't you think?'

'Best crust ever, yes it is the business, Roy.'

'Well, hold out your hand for a second.'

As Harold reached out to me in the dark, I placed a half of Ernie's crust in his hand. He had broken it off Ernie's share of the apple pie, just before he turned out the kitchen light.

'Well done, Roy.'

We both just went silent and had a moment of sheer bliss. Ernie was going to be pretty pissed off, but he would get over it after a couple of years or so. I had a bit of a laugh, so did Harold.

Thursday morning, I hit the front at the dunny queue; nobody there. I ran to the door, jumped in, thinking about my day ahead: payday, payday, payday, you beauty. Don't forget to oil the chain on Harold's bike—it was sounding a little dry in the chain and would slow me down unoiled. Okay, I could hear some voices outside; better get going.

As I was pulling up my shorts, Rita called out through the door, 'Roy don't forget the sawdust.'

I was often a bit lax with the sawdust and knew it was the right thing to do, especially when a young woman was about to use the dunny. I was going to get to work half an hour early because Buster Peters was going to give me a few tips on knife sharpening. He didn't mind sprouting that his knives were the sharpest in the boning room.

Riding through the gates, I gave a wave to Clive the gate man who gave me the nod of approval. 'How is it going Roy?'

'All good Clive!'

'Keep it up Roy!'

'I will!'

As I put my bag on a hook, I thought, *Canteen today that will be good.* I would have to be on my game as the canteen was at the end of the wharf. Shouldn't be a problem.

Buster was at it on the sharpening wheel. Now to look and learn. He passed me one of his knives. It felt well balanced, light. 'Now,' he said, 'with your index finger, try to find an edge on your knife blade. You have to feel each side of the blade. Your nail will catch a small ridge on one side of the blade … can you feel it? Yes, there it is. Well done. Imagine,' said Buster, 'that is the side of the blade that is blunt.' He reached for his sharpening steel hanging off his belt. 'When you run the knife blade up each side of the sharpening steel, rub the side of the blade that has the small ridge that your finger nail caught. Rub that side of the knife first and that will take the ridge off and of course finish off on the same side. Do you understand that? That is lesson one. I will go through the whole thing as we get time. Meanwhile, watch me a bit when you can. As I bone, you will get the gist of the movement on the steel. That will give you a head start.'

'Thanks, Buster.'

'That's okay, Roy, happy to help. You are a good lad.'

'Thanks again, Buster.'

As I was I getting ready for the hooter, I could see Billy up on the boning bench, looking a lot more relaxed and smiling a bit. Maybe he was excited about payday as well.

The noise cranked up and the boners were going hard at it. Someone was singing, loudly. Well, you would not believe it—it was Billy Cummins! He was in full voice, singing 'When Irish Eyes are Shining'. Before you knew it, the whole room was singing. I would never forget it for the rest of my life. Billy was always the man to kick off a song at a wedding or funeral, or birthday.

Finally, lunch time came and Billy and I ran down to the canteen together. You stood in line with a metal tray waiting to be served by ladies with funny half-sized hats pinned into their hair. They looked very efficient, and the range of food behind the counter was a bit bewildering. *What will I have?* I asked myself. Little did I know that this was my first take-away meal.

'Yes lad, what do you want?'

'Well, can I have the sausages and potato and peas, please?'

'Any dessert? Ice cream and jelly.'

'Thank you.' My favourite colours red and green, yum oh.

I didn't know how much it would cost, but as I went to my wallet for some money, the lady serving said that she would put the meal on the tick until next week, after I got my pay.

'What is your name?'

'Roy Holland.'

'What section do you work in?'

'In the boning room.'

'How is Ferpo going?'

'He's well.'

The girls at the other end gave a bit of a giggle. I think Ferpo was a bit of a hit with the girls. He did have a certain persona about him. He was of Spanish descent and kept himself well-groomed. His hair was perfectly combed, jet black and not a grey hair to be seen. He also used Californian Poppy as his hair oil, and that helped keep it perfect at all times.

Billy ordered the same lunch as I did. I must say, even though Mum was a great cook, there was a great sense of satisfaction in the thought that I had ordered a meal from the canteen. I saw Mr O'Boyle sitting over at the window, looking out at the river at the *Belfast Star* tied up at the wharf. His thoughts would have been directed to the *Belfast Star* and all that was going on to make sure that the entire shipment would be processed on time. Reading, yesterday's *Telegraph* newspaper, he had a sort of confidence in his look. He looked up and we caught each other's eye.

'Hello, Roy.'

'Good afternoon sir.'

'All going well?'

'Yes,' I said. 'I am learning how to keep knives.'

'Well that will be handy around here,' he said with a laugh.

We sat a few tables away from Mr O'Boyle, gobbled our lunches down and raced out to get back in time for our restart. Ferpo was standing in the doorway.

'Come on, boys.'

'Yes Ferpo, we're on to it.'

Like a gunshot, the yelling and banging started, and we were into it as well full bore, and before we knew it, we were standing in line with the rest of the men, walking up to a hole in the wall that gave out the pay packets. Billy was behind me. When I stepped up, 'Name,' the pay clerk said.

'Roy Holland.'

And without further ado, the clerk produced a brown packet with my name, my days, my tax. I was so nervous that when I read the top line for tax, I actually thought that ten shillings and sixpence was my amount. Under that was an amount of four pounds, ten shillings and threepence. I stepped back and just kept looking at the pay packet Four pounds, ten shillings and threepence. I was lost for words. I turned to Billy who was, like me, lost for words. We just looked at each other and had a bit of a laugh. I didn't open the packet until I got home and sat on the edge of my bed. I was a bit emotional, and started thinking about the bullying at school. *Fuck 'em*, I thought, *I will make my own way in this life*. I had money now and some things to look forward to—Friday, the end of the working week, and my first swimming lesson with Mr Flemming on Saturday.

I tucked my pay away under my pillow and went downstairs into the backyard. Ginger had her head over the fence. She had that 'I want to go for a ride' look. 'Okay,' I said, 'let's go.' I grabbed my tack from under Dad's shed, saddled up, jumped up and off we both went, not a care in the world.

I have a job, I own a horse.

I had let Choc off his chain, knowing he would also enjoy the run. We moved into a canter up Muir Street toward Naked Gully, called that because most of the kids swam there with no clothes on. We called it 'swimming in the nuddy'.

Life was good.

Chapter 4
A Whole New Life

It was a typical Friday afternoon and I was lying down on my bed. The mattress was filled with kapok; it was a bit lumpy, but it found your shape, and every night you just fitted into your own sleeping position. Our pillows were filled with the same stuffing. Kapok was a poisonous plant that grew wild around the area. When the plant was mature, it would produce dozens of bubbles full of white fluffy seeds that were harvested and stuffed into our bedding. They didn't smell, and the more you gathered, the more comfortable you became in your sleep.

Tonight we had a surprise. We had all put our five shillings in the bottle on top of the fridge. Only eight payments to go and we would own our fridge. Ernie was last to come home, and he was carrying a package, a box made of plywood. Ernie, usually a very quiet, organised person, was very excited as he started opening the package. It all had to be done carefully as he did not want to damage the surprise. Wow! He lifted out our brand new RCA radio, a milky cream colour. It was truly beautiful. We all cheered.

We needed to find a suitable spot so that we could all hear the new radio. It certainly got Dad's attention and he was up suggesting where it could go. The most interesting position was agreed to be the kitchen. After all, it was the spot we all had our meals. The table was in the middle; a sideboard that contained all of our cutlery and plates and so on was beside the fridge, which was positioned near the power point. Ernie was already setting up the radio on the sideboard, plugging it in to the socket behind the fridge. It was ten to seven. The ABC broadcast the world news on the hour every hour, and as a family we could listen to different radio shows, like *Green Bottle,* and Richard Lane's *The Golden Age Of Australian Radio.* As the war was in full swing, it was important to stay up with news about the Yanks making a big impact on progress by slowing up the Japs getting to our shores. The camp down at Creek Road had reached full capacity with a new bunch of eager young Americans, and you could sense that something was about to happen from their part.

With a bit of twitching of the dial on the RCA, we were listening to the news. On our own RCA radio, well done Ernie! He was beaming with pride as the broadcaster read the latest news from around the world.

I was feeling a bit tired and I asked Mum if I could go to bed. I had to be up early the next morning to ride my bicycle to Balmoral to catch the tram to West End to go swimming training with Mr Flemming. Harold said that he would go to bed as well. I didn't know what I might be in for with my first swimming session at seven o'clock at Davies Park pool.

I jumped in to my spot in our bed while Harold did his packing for his train trip tomorrow. He was heading off to the surf club at Tugun and was very excited about his adventure south. None of us had ever seen waves in the ocean, never mind swim in them.

Lying in darkness, Harold and I could hear Mum and Dad laughing in the kitchen at a radio show playing quite loudly. Dad was quite deaf as a result of his time spent in France, with the big artillery guns going off for days on end. A loud radio was a small price to pay for his efforts. The war certainly had destroyed his nervous system and hearing. I always felt lucky that none of us were old enough to be drafted to fight in the war.

Mum had set her alarm clock for five o'clock and this would give me enough time to make the trip to Davies Park pool. With Harold going off to the surf club, it had made me keener than ever to get my swimming up to the standard required to join Harold at Tugun as soon as possible.

At the entrance to the pool, a couple of other boys were standing around with their towels around their necks. I noticed they all looked very fit. A couple were wearing blazers displaying the various badges they had collected. I was doing my best to read what was on the badges. One blazer had the words 'Burleigh Heads Mowbray Park Surf Club' embroidered on the back. I wondered where that was. Little did I know that four years later I would be swimming, stroke for stroke, in an Australian junior surf belt title in Manly, Sydney, against this boy.

There was a rattle at the chain of the gate and a thin, sun-weathered man in his early forties greeted us all. He went into the office and stood behind the open window to take the two bob from each boy to cover the cost of our training session today. I stood back and went through last.

'Good morning, Mr Flemming.'

'Good morning lad. Who are you?'

'I'm Roy Holland. My brother Harold comes here to train with you.'

'Yes, Harold, a good lad.'

'What can I help you with, Roy?'

'Well, I am going to join Tugun Surf Club, and I have to be able to swim four hundred yards in eight minutes to be able to do my bronze medallion in surf lifesaving.'

'Yes, that is true.'

'Can I join your squad?'

'Yes of course, Roy. How often can you come?'

'Well I work at Redbank Abattoir. I knock off around one-thirty in the afternoon and I could ride my bike to Balmoral and catch a tram here to West End Tuesdays, Thursdays and Saturdays.'

'That will be fine. Let me give the squad their instructions, while you go and get your togs on and join me around the pool.'

'Yes, sir.'

I was a bit embarrassed walking around in my togs, but it seemed pretty standard, so I stood beside Mr Flemming until he finished giving his last student his program for his training. There was a blackboard and a hand-painted clock marking sixty seconds. It looked a bit basic but I was sure it would keep all of the squad organised. There were several instructions written in chalk: twenty laps slow, twenty laps medium, and twenty laps hard, with several initials written underneath.

By this time, I was very nervous. All of the swimmers in the pool were swimming with their heads down and I had no idea how to do that. So, rather than embarrass myself, I told Mr Flemming the truth.

'Oh,' he said, 'come over here.'

He asked me to hop up and lie face-down on a two-post stand with a wide flat top. My head was hanging over the front and my arms were dangling down by my side.

'Now Roy, how about you call me Bill? It will be a lot simpler.'

I felt an instant ease come between us now.

'Now the trick to being able to swim long distances with your head down is turning your head to the right and taking a breath. The most important thing is to not tighten up; don't fight the water.'

He held both of my hands out in front of my head while I was lying on his swim stand.

He said, 'Now, as your left hand is entering the water, your right hand is touching your right hip, and your head is turned to the right taking a breath. That is what we are going to practise today. Hop into this lane. Don't dive, just jump in feet first. Now, put your back against the end of the pool, put both your hands out on top of the water, push off and take six strokes with your head down looking at the bottom of the pool.'

'Okay,' I said.

'Don't forget to kick your legs. Ready, go!'

I pushed off and I was quite surprised at how easy it was.

'Very good, Roy. You have good high elbow, which is very important especially when you are swimming in the surf.'

While I was making my way back to the end of the pool, Mr Flemming was calling out instructions to the other members of the squad.

'Now Roy, get yourself ready again. This time, as you push off, practise this: as your left hand enters the water, you turn your head to the right and take a breath. The most important thing is when you turn your head to look back at the bottom of the pool you blow out all of the air ready for the next breath. Give it a go.'

Well, I will never forget my excitement as I finished off my second attempt.

'Thankyou Bill. I get it.'

'Now have a go at one length of the pool, and don't rush it. Every time your left hand enters the water, turn your head to the right and take a breath. And don't forget the most important thing: blow out the air, or you won't be able to keep your timing.'

'Thanks, Bill.'

'Your target today is eight laps, one at a time.'

'Okay, I'll give it a go.'

My first lap was a bit exhausting and Bill called out to me to relax and not fight the water. 'If you don't relax, the water will win every time. That's better,' he called out as I finished my second lap. 'Take your time.'

After I had completed my third lap, I was really getting the rhythm, understanding that the blowing out of the air was the key to rhythm. Somehow, I completed my eighth lap and I was absolutely stuffed. Mr Flemming said that I had done well and that he wanted me to sit in the stands and watch the other swimmers, to get some idea of how a training session is done. The session lasted about an hour and a half, then Mr Flemming asked everybody to hop out of the pool and gather in a group at the canteen where we could buy a glass of cordial and get to know each other. I met Barry Johns.

'Where are you from, Roy?'

'Cannon Hill.'

'Ah, you are Harold's brother.'

'Yes,' I said. 'What's your name?'

'Barry Johns,' was his reply. I had noticed him in the water. He was a great swimmer, with his high elbows seeming to glide through the water. Barry asked where I worked and I responded with, 'Redbank.'

'What section?'

'Boning room.'

'How's Ferpo?'

'He's well. I have only worked there for a week, but I am enjoying it and the money is good. Where do you work, Barry?'

'I am on the beef kill floor.'

'Have you been there long?'

'About three years. Takes a bit of getting used to.' he said, 'but the work is consistent and the money is also good. You should probably get a bit older and a bit more experienced with the whole process. The violence of the place can be extreme.'

I said that I had settled into the boning room well and expected to stay there for a good while to come.

'Good,' Barry said. 'It has taken me years to be able to deal with it as just a job.'

And that, I thought, *is all it is. A job, just like the dunny man back home. It is just a job, a means to an end. We all have families to provide for. That's what it's all about.*

'Well, boys,' Mr Flemming addressed his charges who were deep in conversation on various topics ranging from catching waves at their respective surf club to their current girlfriend. This was all very new to me.

'Boys, stop your chattering and listen. For those of you that haven't met our new swimmer, his name is Roy Holland.'

I felt a certain lift with the words 'Roy Holland swimmer', and on those words the boys gave me a welcome clap, and all came over and shook my hand.

'Well, I will see you all on Tuesday afternoon, three o'clock sharp.'

'Thanks, Bill,' they all responded.

On that we all found our way out and went on our way. Some of the boys had motor cars and a couple had motor bikes with sidecars. Barry had a sidecar and called out to me if I needed a lift.

'Yes,' I said, 'I am off to the tram to go back to Balmoral.'

'Oh, I live with my Mum at Bulimba, the next suburb. Get in.'

We peeled back the protective cover on the sidecar.

'Hop in, Roy. Put these cap and goggles on, sit down, shut up and hold on.'

Barry wore a brown leather jacket and a matching cap and goggles. He really looked the part. He gave the seven-fifty Norton a stiff kick with his right boot and the bike roared into life. I was absolutely terrified. This was all new ground for me. Barry dropped the bike into first gear, and the next thing we were roaring down Melbourne Street in South Brisbane at what seemed a hundred miles an hour. Barry was an excellent rider, or at least I hoped he was. Sitting in a sidecar with no control of your future was a huge blood rush. I had a grip on the sidecar that could hold an elephant. Over the beautiful Victoria Bridge, again at top speed, heading up to the Albion Fiveways, across Wickham Terrace and down into the Valley. Wow this was fun; we were going over the Story Bridge.

Barry yelled out, 'No fat-arse coppers around here!' and on that dropped the Norton back a couple of gears and we were flat out. Barry was really getting into it. As we came off the Story Bridge, Barry roared through and around the toll gate. The gateman didn't seem to mind; in fact he gave Barry a big wave. As we drifted around the left-hand sweeper, I felt the sidecar lift off the ground for a short distance, much to Barry's excitement. I had never enjoyed myself so much, ever.

Not long after, Barry was pulling up at my tram stop where I had pushed my bike into the bushes to hide it. As I climbed out, I got a dose of the wobbly legs, and almost fell out of the sidecar. As I was putting the skull cap and goggles back into the sidecar, Barry said, 'I will see you again on Tuesday and we can do the same thing.'

Shit, I thought, *I will be doing this a bit more often.* I couldn't wait to tell Dad about it because he loved motor bikes. *Maybe Barry would give Dad a burn around the block down the track. Dad would never forget it I am sure.*

I jumped up on my bike and rode home at breakneck speed, imagining that I was riding my own Norton and sidecar. It was about five miles from Balmoral to home, and after the eight laps I did at swimming training, I walked slowly up the front stairs—running was not an option. I was feeling pretty stuffed.

Harold was not home. Of course he was on his way to Tugun Surf Club and the others were not at home either. Dad was up robbing the bees and Mum was at church in Keats Street Cannon Hill. Mum's church gathered on Saturday. I don't remember what denomination the gathering was but they met on Saturdays after lunch. I had never been, and Mum had given up on all of us, as we were not remotely interested. Too many things on the go, I guess. I went to the fridge for any leftovers. Great, some cold baked potatoes and pumpkin. I grabbed a handful and ripped into them, without leaving a tooth mark in them. I was so hungry. Then I thought I might put my head down for a little catnap. I don't even remember my head hitting the pillow.

'Roy, wake up boy.'
    Dad was standing over me coaxing me to wake up.
    'Yes Dad, what is it ?'
    'I wondered if you wanted to go fishing over at the river.'
    'Have you got any bait?'
    'Yes,' he said excitedly.
    'What sort?'
    'Tom brought some congealed blood and some spinal cord from the beef kill yesterday.'
    'Yes, let's go; maybe catch some sea mullet from under the wharfs.'
    'How about we put Ginger behind the sulky in the shed? I greased the axles, all should be okay.'
    'Good idea, Dad. I'll get my favourite fishing line and float and meet you with Ginger up in the shed. Can Choc come?'
    'Yes, try leaving without him.'

I decided to let Dad have the reins as Ginger was a bit impatient. She also was looking forward to the adventure.

'I'll get the gate, Dad.'

'Good, Roy. I'll meet you on the street.'

I raced down the side of the house and opened the gate. Dad was very experienced with harness travel. Things had changed with the introduction of motor cars and motorbikes in the last twenty years. I closed the gate behind Dad and Ginger, and of course Choc was sitting on the ground beside Dad waiting for Dad's call.

'Okay, Choc, up, up.'

On that, Choc jumped up and into the back of the sulky. Choc was beside himself happy running around and around inside the sulky. Dad gave him the big 'shut up and lie down!' Choc got the message and settled in for the trip.

Our destination was Baines Wharf, over at the Brisbane River. The wharf was beside Redbank Abattoir, and because of the volume of offal that was dumped into the river every weekday, it was a natural draw for all sorts of edible fish species—mullet, bream, and John Dory. We had no problem with the environment that the fish had come from. The wharf was abandoned and had been for a few years after the original slaughter house had been abandoned, and after Redbank Meatworks, where I worked, had been established.

We parked Ginger and the sulky in the shade of a stand of date palms that had a large patch of fresh kikuyu grass under it. Ginger wouldn't wander far from a good chew of fresh kikuyu grass.

'Come on, Dad, two bob says I get the first mullet.'

'You're on,' said Dad. He seemed to lose about twenty years at the thought of catching a big mullet.

As Dad and I walked away from the stand of date palms, carrying our fishing gear, I could see the remnants of old boilers and killing pens that had for years been a thriving slaughter house. I could sense the terror that would have been the end of the line of so many animals' lives. I did sometimes think hard about what, if any, emotions condemned animals might feel. Best to keep walking.

Dad was setting a good pace, as he wanted to be the one to catch the first mullet, and get me for two bob. Our mission was to crawl our way around on the massive horizontal timber structure under the wharf then bait up our handlines with the congealed strips of cattle blood. The art was to float your bait as close as possible to the barnacle-encrusted vertical timber piles, and wait for that wonderful hit of a large sea mullet as it grabbed the baited hook. All hell would break loose as you did your best to stop the mullet from wrapping itself around the pile and breaking off.

We had to force our way under the wharf gate and of course around the 'Danger No Entry' sign, which, as Dad said, was a waste of money. We climbed down a metal ladder and soon we were making our way along myriad horizontal beams that held all of the wharf piles vertical. We had our favourite spot where we could sit side by side and fish together. We set ourselves up and Dad's line and float was first to hit the water. The mullet were used to eating the strips of solid blood. Dad and I were both very competitive, and jockeying for the best float position was always great fun.

Bugger, Dad has hooked one, a big one. His fish was trying its best to tangle his line around the pile, but Dad was up to the task. The trick was to get the mullet's head out of the water, and Dad did it. Next he had to pull the fish up the twelve or so feet to his chest where he could grab it and slip his fingers into its gills.

'Good work, Dad!' I yelled. 'That is a beauty. Well there goes my hard-earned two shillings.'

Dad, laughed out loud with much excitement. 'Yes it does, Roy.'

On that, my line went off. Boy oh boy, this was also a big fish. Same deal as Dad—head out, pull it up and on to my chest.

'Good fishing, Roy.'

'Thanks, Dad.'

Two fish in the bag, and we couldn't wait till dinner. We caught a couple more and decided we'd had enough.

'Let's leave some for next time.'

'Good idea.'

Back over our steps and back to Ginger and the sulky. Ginger had eaten a large patch of grass, and I hoped she would not be too full. I had tied Choc up in the back of the sulky because he would have been a pain in the arse if we hadn't. Choc was very excited to see us but Ginger did not share the same enthusiasm. She needed some extra persuasion to get her into a trot.

I have said it before, life was good.

Dad was looking forward to filleting the mullet and presenting the fish to Mum for her to wave her magic over it. Mum would dip the fillets in a beer batter before cooking them in the pan with fresh dripping until they were golden brown. They'd be accompanied by some of Mum's pre-cooked potato chips dug from Dad's potato patch.

Rita and Tom would be home for dinner before going to the dance at the local dance hall at seven o'clock. Tom would probably have a couple of beers with Dad over dinner and then get a chance to sharpen his fighting skills at the dance.

Dad did a great job filleting the mullet, and as we sat down for Saturday dinner together, the six o'clock news came on the radio. The war with Japan was the main story. The Australian defence forces were going to build a defensive line around Brisbane in an effort to protect the city from a possible Japanese invasion. Mum was very upset by this news, but Dad reassured her that all would be well.

After the magnificent fish and chips, I was ready for bed so I excused myself. I had things to think about. For example, I was not convinced that I could meet the deadline of the end of March to swim four hundred yards in eight minutes to qualify to join the Tugun Surf Club as a junior member and wondered if the goal I had set myself was realistic. As I sat on my bed that night, I decided I might be better off concentrating on work and making sure that I became a good swimmer rather than a basher. I would give myself until October before trying to qualify for the surf club. After all, that would be the beginning of a new surf season and I would be fourteen by then. I had a plan—enjoy work and training, and hopefully get the chance to have some more trips home in the sidecar with Barry Johns.

The months passed quickly and before I knew it, Mum was putting the finishing touches to another birthday cake. I couldn't believe I had been working for almost a year already! Mum had given strict instructions to the rest of the family to be home by six. I had skipped swimming training as I didn't want to miss any of my birthday. I had been working with Dad in his potato patch. He could no longer dig with the garden fork, because his lungs were losing their strength from his experiences in the war. Mum had cooked oxtail stew using three oxtails I had smuggled out in my bag. They were not a popular piece at the boning room, and all of us took home our share. Mum, of course, cooked them in the pressure cooker. I don't know how she got the gravy so rich. We had mashed potato and fresh green peas which were fantastic. Dad, of course, was at the head of the table and insisted that we listen to the six o'clock news headlines. The bloody Japs were not far away and were bombing Darwin. Twenty-six Aussies were killed in one air raid. Fortunately, General MacArthur was well set up here in Brisbane, and the US Army camp at Creek Road was at full strength.

'Don't worry Minnie, the Yanks will sort things out. Remember this, you kids. In warfare, never attack; always defend. Defenders are always more organised on home soil.'

The oxtails were fantastic and now it was my turn. Mum called us all to come and sit down and celebrate my fourteenth birthday. Rita turned the kitchen light off and Mum entered the kitchen with a vanilla cream sponge cake complete with fourteen lit candles. The family sang 'Happy Birthday', with Dad as usual wanting to have the final say. Hip hip hooray

'Now Roy, Mum and I want to thank you for your financial input into the buying of the Kelvinator fridge. What a great family effort the fridge turned out to be. Mum and I are very proud of you all. Well done.'

On that, Ernie piped in to say that we had just paid our September payment and that was the last payment so we now owned the fridge. A great cheer went up and Mum started the rally again for 'Happy Birthday'. Her youngest boy was fourteen years of age and she was not going to let the moment slip. Our singing rang loud throughout the house. 'Hip hip hooray, quick Roy blow those candles out, the icing is about to melt!' One almighty blow and we were in darkness. The cake was outstanding, of course, the milk and cream coming from Jessey our home cow.

I gave Mum a special hug, to which she responded with a gentle kiss on the cheek. On that, I was off to bed. I wondered how Harold was going down at the surf club. I missed him, and our goodnight talks. Harold had a great heart. With a job as a journeyman carpenter, he would be away this winter working, building fences out west on a large cattle property at Goondiwindi. *It's funny where life takes you if you let it,* I thought. *Fourteen years old today. I think this coming year will be different, swimming, surf club, motor bikes, Ferpo Neumann.*

My boss at the boning room wanted me to think about going and learning the trade of beef butcher. I asked if Billy could come. Ferpo said of course. Billy and I were getting to know a lot of the other workers, and a lot of banter went on between us all. I learnt very early not to take myself too seriously, and so did Billy. He and I would be friends for life, I knew it.

'Well, Ferpo, we really like it here, and it hasn't even been a full year since we started.'

'Yes, I know,' he said, 'but a couple of positions have come up, and they are permanent jobs, and better pay, and the other good thing is I won't have to look at you two ugly bastards anymore.'

I could tell that Ferpo was trying to do the best for us two, and would be glad to see us get on.

'Oh and don't forget, you will have to make some adjustments. This boning room is like a kindergarten compared to the kill floor. Just remember ...', but before he could continue I said, 'It's only a job, remember the dunny man.' Ferpo gave a big loud laugh.

'So that's it; you two start Monday. Report to Chooka Lewis. He is a bit of a character, but a good butcher. I know you will get on with him.'

'Chooka Lewis, okay Ferpo, and thank you for the start.'

'That's okay, boys.'

Billy and I went to the showers. We were both getting used to the open shower where nobody seemed to care about nudity. We all just showered, got dressed and left.

Winter was slowly starting to leave us. I had forgotten, to count winter into my calculation for training at Mr Flemming's swimming squad. Tomorrow I would be back in the pool to continue on with my quest to swim four hundred yards in eight minutes.

Harold was due back from a fencing job out west. He had absolutely fallen on his feet down at Tugun, and he was off on the train to the coast in the morning. He was cutting it fine with his arrival back home, but he would do whatever was necessary to ensure that he didn't miss the seven-thirty train on Saturday morning. At this point, I didn't know what drew him to Tugun beach. One thing I did know was that I was going to swimming training tomorrow morning with a clear and precise mission—eight minutes for swimming four hundred yards. Same drill as when we all broke up for winter.

Mr Flemming looked rested and ready to go.

'Now boys, we are going to have some stroke correction across the pool before we start. It will take some time to sort out, but it will be a starting point for our long year together. Let's put you top five swimmers at the far end working our way down. Please Roy, don't take this personally, but you will be at this end close to me. Remember boys, keep your head looking across the pool not up in the air when you turn your head to take your breath. Okay Roy, remember blow out your air when your face is looking at the bottom of the pool.'

'Yes Bill.'

'Okay, in you get.'

As we hit the water it was as cold as snow. This was not in my calculation for improving my speed in the pool. After a while of swimming across the pool, things became bearable. Bill was getting me to swim with my head down. I was a bit rusty, a bit embarrassed actually, but Bill's manner around the pool was very reassuring and I grew in confidence with his attitude.

'Okay boys,' he yelled. 'All of you top swimmers, look at the training board and get on with it. Roy come over here in the shallow end, back against the wall. Okay Roy, push off and give me six strokes with your head down, no breathing at this point. Okay, ready … go. Yes Roy, that is good. Now come back and try left hand enters the water head turns to the right and takes a breath.'

'Got it Bill.'

'Very good Roy, fantastic high elbows. Let's try for eight laps this time. I want you to do two laps at a time not one. Take your time, don't rush it.'

I got the first two laps, but was absolutely stuffed. What Bill didn't know was that I had taken up smoking. Most of the men at work smoked, so it was a social thing, but I could certainly feel the difference from when I stopped swimming till now. I struggled through my laps as instructed, but really fell short as I finished off my last lap. Bill was standing at the end of the pool looking down at me as I touched the end of the pool.

'What the hell have you been doing to yourself Roy?'

I looked up at him. He knew something was wrong and got me to get out of the pool and meet him away a bit from the pool edge, in an effort for us to get some privacy.

'Well Roy, what's new?'

'I took up smoking over the winter break.'

Bill was clearly pissed off. 'Roy,' he said, 'when you came to me your target was to swim four hundred yards in eight minutes. I took you seriously; that is why I committed myself to you. I am not going to lecture on the pros and cons of smoking, but I will not be mucked around. If you are serious, you need to go back, take a look deep into yourself and lift yourself above the other workers at your job. You don't have to make a big deal out of it; just, look at yourself and *say I want to be different I want* to be a surf life saver at Tugun. So finish up now, don't get a lift back to Balmoral with Barry, walk up to the tram and think out where you want to be. And take steps to give smoking the flick.'

I was almost emotional. Because of his sincerity, Bill had got in to my core, something I had never experienced. '

'Thanks Bill, can I come back Tuesday?'

'Yes of course, get back into your push-ups before work.'

'I will, Bill.'

We shook hands and I was holding myself together as best I could.

'Roy, I will sort things out with Barry regarding your lift okay?'

'Thanks again Bill.'

'Okay, I will see you Tuesday.'

Chapter 5
Vigilance and Service 1945

The day had finally come for me to attempt to qualify for my swim time for four hundred yards. Mum was up making me a special breakfast—porridge with fresh cream from Jessey and some of Dad's honey. Harold had stayed home from Tugun to come and give me support.

Down the back stairs, Harold had a great surprise. He had bought a new, cream FJ Holden from the extra money he earnt building boundary fences out west. He tooted the horn, and I got the gate. Harold was a good driver, steady on the gears, although I didn't understand the principles of the driving bit. I would learn a lot from Harold as he was very patient, and he would teach me well.

We were going up Morningside Hill, and Harold tooted the horn to the old police sergeant who had pulled another driver over, probably giving him a speeding ticket. The sarge gave us a wave back. I looked back at the old copper, and I was concerned that the old sarge was still waving his arms in the air, looking at us disappearing away from him. Harold had only just got his licence a couple of days ago.

'Shit!' Harold said. 'We better slow down.' The speed limit was thirty-five miles an hour. I chirped in to say that maybe the copper was wanting us to stop as well, as we were doing forty. Harold hit the accelerator and we pulled up at Davies Park Pool without the coppers behind us. All good for now. There were a lot more people there than I had expected. As I got out of the Holden, I could hear Barry's Norton motorbike turning into the street. He was very proud of the new exhaust system that he'd had fitted during the week, and as he got halfway down the street toward us, all heads turned to have a look at what was making all the noise. Barry did a fantastic U-turn manoeuvre that got a big cheer from the crowd.

I was very nervous. 'Good day, Harold.'

'You too, Roy.'

'Big day, Roy.'

'Yes,' I said nervously.

'Good day, Bill.'

'Good to see you, boys. All sleep well, did we?'

A few moans and groans came from the other boys. They knew when he asked if we'd slept well that he knew that most of them had either been out drinking or in the cot with their girlfriends for most of the night. *Well,* I thought, *that will be me soon, down at the surf club.* But first things first. Four hundred yards in eight minutes today. I found my way over and stood with two other boys that were attempting the same swim. Their names were Noel and Brian. Mr Flemming was getting up some of the stragglers that obviously were a bit hung over. One of them, of course, was Barry. He really knew how to enjoy himself on a Friday night at the Bulimba pub.

Once they were all in the pool doing their swimming program, a short solid man dressed in his Tugun Surf Lifesaving Club blazer came over to join us.

'My name is Harry Harsley, boys, and I am the chief instructor of the Tugun Surf Club.'

He started thanking us for our efforts so far, and a special thank you of course to Bill. 'Your efforts are greatly appreciated in getting the lads to this point.'

On that, we gave Bill a well-deserved hand clap. I reflected on how far I had come under Bill's guidance. I was swimming smoothly and had given up the fags.

Bill was touched by the comments.

'Now, this time trial is all about saving lives, including your own. Swimming through waves down at Tugun is an exhausting experience, especially in big surf conditions, and if someone is drowning, it is you that will have to swim out, pulling a surf line to save them from drowning. It's a big responsibility.' He continued, 'If all goes well today, and you qualify, then the surf club will formally ask you down to the clubhouse at Tugun to train to get your bronze medallion. So I would like to point out that today hopefully will be your first step in becoming a surf lifesaver. You have to do this swimming test every year to make sure that you stay proficient. Our motto is "Vigilance and Service", and the public rely on us to be surf-ready whenever the opportunity arises. Any questions?'

'No, Harry, thank you,' we said. I didn't realise how big a responsibility this was. Harry asked who wanted to go first. The three of us were a bit pensive, so Harry picked Noel to go first.

'The rules are you can have a bit of a breather if you need it, but your feet must not touch the bottom of the pool, or you will be disqualified and have to come back next year. Remember to pace yourself—eight minutes for eight laps. Okay, Noel, it is a diving start. I have the stopwatch that will give the exact time. If I think you are swimming at a speed that won't get you to finish on time, I will call out to you so you know.'

Noel nodded. 'Okay, Noel, take your mark, get set, go!'

On that, Noel hit the water. He was going well. Not as tall as us other two, he had a shorter stroke. Noel was at the six-lap stage, turning, with two laps to go. As he turned, Harry called out go harder. Noel heard his call, and you could see him putting all he had in his tank to get to the other end of the pool and back again. Harry was hanging over the end of the pool to ensure that the time clock was stopped at precisely the time of Noel's arrival at the end of the pool.

'It is going to be close,' Harry called out.

As Noel hit the wall, we all held our breath: seven minutes and fifty-two seconds. He had done it. Noel, absolutely stuffed, got out of the pool and was congratulated by all of us. He had a grin on his face that said it all.

'Well done, Noel, you qualify.'

'Thanks Harry,' Noel said.

'Now, Roy Holland, your turn.'

Bill came over to me and said in a quiet voice, 'I want you to go steady; get your breathing going and stretch out; no bashing, got it?'

'Yes, Bill.'

'Okay, Roy, good luck. Take your mark, get set, go.'

In I went, remembering Bill's instructions. I felt strong, and I was stretching out. Four laps down, and I thought I was going all right until I heard Harry call out, 'Go faster.'

Wow. I had better get my finger out. I stepped up the pace but still kept my smooth stroke going, turning for the last lap. I felt good and was going to give this last lap a big go. Bill had told me in earlier sessions to keep my head down and finish hard for the final six strokes. Bang, I hit the wall.

Harry was smiling, so I knew I was in with a chance. 'Seven minutes and ten seconds. Well done, Roy.'

The others gathered around and offered well-done handshakes. 'Well, Roy, you will get a chance to join our junior rescue and resuscitation team with a time like that.'

I had no idea what that all meant, but it sounded good. Now it was up to Brian to make it a clean sweep.' Brian got himself ready.

Soon Brian was in the water, going as hard as he could. At two laps to go, I saw old Harry move over to the end of the pool, where Brian was about to turn for his final two laps. 'Go harder!' he yelled. Old Harry was getting a bit excited by the fact that Brian was close to running out of time. You could see that Brian was giving his all. Old Harry started walking beside Brian, yelling words of encouragement. As Brian turned for the last lap, old Harry screamed at his swimmer to go hard, six strokes to go. Old Harry yelled out again, 'Go hard!'

Bang, Brian had finished, and again we all held our breath for the result. You would not believe it—seven minutes and fifty-eight seconds. We all raced over, and Harry showed us the stop watch. 'Seven minutes and fifty-eight. Well boys, welcome to Tugun Surf Club, and it is my shout for the raspberry cordials. What do you think Bill?'

'I agree. Boys, well done.'

'Thank you again Bill.'

By the time the three of us filled out our application forms to join the surf club, all of the other boys were climbing out of the pool after completing their respective training sessions. I was on a high; the whole morning had been a great introduction to the next phase of our lives together and we now realised how serious surf lifesaving was and what was expected of each of us. Old Harry said his goodbyes, and Harold my brother came over to shake our hands. He was a bit tired after his training session.

'Well, come on Roy,' Harold said. 'Let's go up to the Lighthouse Café at the top of town and have a celebration—chocolate malted milks and hamburgers to go with them. Old Harry called out to us as we headed across to Harold's new car, which by now had been surrounded by most of the swimmers. 'Boys, I forgot to give you your Tugun shirts.' On that, he produced three emerald green collared shirts, with 'Tugun Surf Lifesaving Club' embroidered on the left chest in gold letters. 'They cost six shillings, but you can pay me down at the clubhouse at Tugun when you like.'

Harold insisted that we put our new shirts on. I now felt that I was going to be a surf lifesaver. Somehow, Brian and Noel were in the back seat of our car. On we went, next stop the Lighthouse Cafe. It was nine o'clock on Saturday morning, the 16th of December 1944. Harold parked the Holden right outside the cafe. Wow, the place was packed, and I was as pleased as punch with all of us wearing our Tugun shirts. We got a few looks from some of the local lads, and there was a table or two with four girls sitting, smiling, doing everything they could to look as uninterested as possible, but somehow you knew that they were. We jumped onto a table as a couple of regulars vacated their seats. There was music playing, a man singing on the radio quite loudly. Harold said that the man singing was Bing Crosby and the song was 'White Christmas'. I liked it but with all the yelling and squalling by the girls, it all seemed normal. We were super excited, and a young waitress came and took our order. This was all very new to me; things that I had never seen or heard. Harold said that he was going down the coast to Tugun next weekend and did we want to go. I jumped in and said *yes*, and the other two could not get *yes* out quick enough.

'If you like, now we have the car, we can leave Friday arvo about three o'clock at our place. We can all chip in to pay for the petrol if that suits.'

'Yes, of course we will,' I chirped in.

'You'll need a couple of towels and shorts and shirts and don't forget your togs, and of course your Tugun shirt. We'll go out to the beach house at Coolangatta.'

'Coolangatta, where is that, Harold?'

'Well, it is where the train from Brisbane line ends at the New South Wales border. There are several guesthouses on the beach. That's where all the good looking sheilas stay.'

Wow! Noel was smiling; Noel had a great smile! You could tell that he was very excited by the way his left leg was jiggling and the table was vibrating.

'Sounds great!'

I could hardly contain myself.

The burgers and milkshakes arrived and, boy did they taste good! I even got a little smile from a young girl sitting across from us. She looked beautiful, and I noticed she was wearing a nurse's uniform. The women's hospital was not far away, and they must have worked the night shift.

'Well, boys,' Harold said, 'let's get out of here. Noel and Brian, I will drop you off at your homes, and Roy and I are going home to wash the car.'

'Great idea. Harold, can I do the windows?'

'Sure you can.'

As we jumped in the car to leave, that little girl in the nurse's uniform gave me another smile, and I felt a little pang in my stomach. I smiled back. *Wow*, I thought, and then turned my attention back to my mates. There were a few other boys that were admiring the FJ Holden, just standing looking and dreaming. Harold was beaming with pride. In we got, and off we went. As we approached the Story Bridge on the southern side, I looked to my left and could see the Eagers Holden new car showroom, where there were several new Holdens for sale, gleaming at me from behind the crystal clear glass. *I want one* I thought.

I was starting on the beef kill floor with Bill Cummings in a couple of weeks, and I was a bit tight in the gut thinking about the step-up in responsibilities.

Half an hour later, Harold and I were in the kitchen at the table. Dad was reading the Saturday paper and enjoying a cup of tea with Mum. We two boys were still very excited and were telling Mum about my swim.

'I'm very proud of you both,' Mum said.

As Dad was reading the section of the newspaper dedicated to the war, he commented on the fact that the Normandy offensive had been an overwhelming result for the Allies and that France had been liberated. I guess Dad was a bit confused that some twenty-odd years earlier he had been sweating it out digging trenches on the Somme in France. 'I can still hear the roar of those bloody cannons as they blasted their shells from a standing start, off into the darkness to terrorise God knows what.' I could see Dad's eyes get a little glazed.

Mum was quick to get up from her chair and give Dad a soft hug of support. 'Thank you, Minnie,' he said. Mum had a wonderful soft nature, and her touch on Dad's forehead was a beautiful expression of love and understanding for Dad's torture on the battlefields during the war. Mum had met Dad after his tour of the Somme. Battle-weary from extensive gassing, he had been sent back to London for treatment. After he was discharged from hospital, and before returning to Australia, he visited his old home in Yorkshire. While he was in the backyard, a beautiful young woman popped her head over the fence. 'Hi, I'm Minnie.' And things blossomed from there.

Before long, Dad was on his feet. 'Okay, you boys, time to get on with washing that car, but just make sure you don't make a boghole in the backyard from too much water. We are a little bit short of water at the moment; the tanks are about half-full so limit yourself to a couple of buckets.'

'No problem, Dad. Can I put my car under the dunny shed up the back?'

'I am sorry Harold but Tom has beaten you to it. He is bringing his new Zephyr home in a couple of weeks. You could probably find some room under the house, I think.'

'Roy and I will sort things out after we wash the car.'

On that, Harold and I were into detailing the Holden.

On Friday afternoon, I said goodbye to all my mates in the boning room. After my first weekend down at Tugun Surf Club, I would be starting my training as a butcher. I had mixed feelings about leaving the boning room but I knew that the new job opportunity was going to be for the good and I got plenty of support from my mates in the boning room. Monday was going to be interesting.

Riding home that day, I accepted that my life was going to take some new directions and I was excited. As I got off my pushbike at home, there was plenty going on. Harold, Noel and Brian were busy packing the FJ, ready to head off to the coast. I had already packed my bag and had showered at work so just a matter of putting on my Tugun shirt, a pair of shorts and my leather sandals. A quick kiss for Mum and we were off: next stop, Tugun Surf Club.

'How long, Harold?'

'About three hours, depending on traffic.'

'How fast can we go?'

'Well, on the open road, it is sixty miles an hour, but I drive at fifty, to be safe. We will get there soon enough.'

I was a bit tired, and the boys in the back had slowed up a bit with their barrage of questions, like 'What do we eat?'

Harold said that there was a kitchen and dining hall and that an old shearers' cook called Jack lived at the clubhouse.

'Make sure you get on well with Jack.'

'Why is that, Harold?'

'Well, old Jack has been known to slide a dead cockroach or two under your mashed potatoes. You don't see it until you are halfway through your meal. Be warned; manners are the key.'

I decided to make sure that I checked things out before I got stuck into my meals.

'How much is a meal?'

'One shilling.'

'Oh, that is cheap,' I said.

'You pay for your meals on Saturday morning. Three meals a day, as you will need all the food you can get. The days are exhausting—swimming and bronze medallion training. The senior members can get a bit tough at times. They like to make sure that the incoming new members are hard enough to carry on with the Tugun tradition. Down at the local dances, don't take a backward step in defending our surf club.'

I guessed my boxing skills would help me gain a little respect.

'Whatever you do, just keep your head down and don't be a smart arse or you will pay for it dearly, I assure you. Coming up to Beenleigh, boys. Will we get a Yatala pie each? Get the mushy peas and black sauce. We won't eat in the car, though; too many crumbs.'

'Oh, okay.'

I ordered my pie and sat down at a timber picnic table with the rest of my mates. As I opened the paper bag, I was looking at the most magnificent, golden, crisp, flaky pastry, piping hot, just-out-of-the-oven, meat pie.

'How good is this?' Harry said as we crunched our way through the pie. It was that good you had to be careful to keep your fingers out of the way, or you could easily do yourself some damage. A bottle of chocolate milk to wash it down.

'Well boys, that was dinner,' Harold said jokingly. 'Shake all the crumbs off before you get in the car, and let's go. I wasn't going to stop at the pie shop, but the temptation was too strong, and I just had to have a Yatala pie with mushy peas.'

Harold had a radio, and music was playing; songs that I had never heard before, but I liked them. We were driving over the Southport Bridge.

'What a beautiful spot,' I called out as we came to the end of the bridge. Harold told us that the building on our left was Southport Surf Club. I could not see the ocean or any waves yet, but Harold said that we were coming up to a place where we would see waves. It was called Narrow Neck.

And there it was. We all called out 'wow' and chattered with excitement at the waves crashing onto the shore. I looked, stunned in amazement. Harold said that the waves at this end of the coast were a heavier wave and not as good for catching a body wave. You could get a real dumping out there.

'I can't wait till we get to Tugun,' Noel said loudly.

'That's Burleigh Heads Surf Club on our left, and see out at that point? That is a great spot for catching waves on surf skis.'

'What are they?' Brian said.

'Well, they are made of plywood, and you sit on them and paddle with a wooden paddle. You'll soon be at the clubhouse, and this is Tallebudgera Bridge, nice spot, crystal clear water.'

I said, 'I bet we can catch some fish there.'

'We are making good time, just one more bridge at Currumbin.'

'Cripes, all these unusual names. I will never remember them.'

'Yes, you will.'

As we came over the last hill and down onto a stretch of flat road, we did a left then a right.

'Well boys, we are here, Tugun Surf Club.' Harold drove up to the weatherboard building. 'Massive pine trees,' I said.

Harold said that they were Norfolk Island pines.

We pulled up. It had taken us two hours and forty-five minutes to get here, including the pie stop. The wind was blowing a bit as we each grabbed our carry bags. We were wearing our Tugun shirts, which gave me a bit of confidence as we walked through the front doors. I looked up at the wall to my left and spotted an honour board hanging on the wall. It had names of all of the office bearers that had served their club for past generations. I could not help but notice that Harold's name was on the board for last year as Vice-Captain. I didn't know that! Harold was a very private person and never talked it up.

We climbed up a winding set of timber stairs. As we were going up, a couple of young blokes ran down the stairs at breakneck speed. Harold yelled out to them, 'Where are you two going?'

'For a swim,' they yelled back.

As we got to the top of the stairs, I looked forward and through a large timber-framed window in the half-light of sundown, I could see the two young blokes running down towards the water. The waves were big far out but smaller in close to the shore. Harold took us over to some double-decker bunks and appointed us to a bunk each.

'Okay, these are your bunks from here on,' Harold said. 'Hey boys, put your bathers on and let's get wet.'

Why not? I thought. I was used to the nudity thing, so I pulled off my clothes, jumped into my bathers, grabbed a towel from my bag, and we too were running down to the beach. I will never forget my first few steps on Tugun beach. The sand was cold and soft, like nothing I had felt before, I ran and jumped around like a kid that had just been given his first present. Harold was in the lead. I must say, I did not know what I was

A reelman: how Roy and his young friends rescued the young girl.

Young lifesavers stand proudly before the reel.

A bronze whaler, the most common man-eater found in the area.

The train that used to run from Brisbane to Coolangatta.

Longboards typical of this era.

in for, but I thought I would hold back and let Harold show us the ropes. I ran into the water and dived. The saltwater tasted beautiful. We swam out about thirty yards and grouped ourselves together, duck-diving, dog paddling, just letting it all out. I felt a sense of home. As I looked back up the beach at the clubhouse, I realised that I now had a second home.

'It's getting dark,' Harold called out. 'Sharks get hungry at this time of day. Early morning and late afternoon is their feeding time.'

Shit, did he say sharks? I didn't read this in the contract.

As we walked back to the showers, I quizzed Harold about the shark bit.

'Yes,' he said, 'there are several attacks each year at the beaches north and south of us. A beach called Kirra—three beaches south of here—they have had several shark attacks.'

We all went a bit quiet. *Sharks, sharks, sharks* were all I could think of.

We were in the showers and enthusiasm had picked up a bit.

'I am a bit hungry,' Noel said.

'We'll go to the Tugun pub. They have great T-bone steaks and chips for two shillings, including a pot of beer.'

'That is me,' I said. Back on with the shorts and shirt and two hundred and thirty-eight paces later, we were ordering our T-bone and chips. A couple of senior members had joined us, and we were all introduced. The seniors were a bit drunk, but no one seemed to care; it all seemed normal. As our steaks arrived, I looked down at my steak and wondered if we had met before … didn't matter. Great streaks, but the chips were not as good as Mum's. I had my first beer at the Tugun pub. *It would not be the last*, I thought.

It had been a big day for all of us, but as Harold pointed out, it was only Saturday tomorrow. Making the extra effort to get down there on a Friday arvo was worth it.

Harold was patrol captain on the beach in the morning at eight o'clock, and he asked if we could join him to start to get an understanding of the goings-on of beach life.

Lying in my wire-framed bunk bed, I could hear the crashing of the waves. It was quite loud. I was looking forward to the morning but feeling still a bit concerned about the shark attacks. I was sure that when I was in the surf in the morning, I would be on the lookout for anything that resembled a shark. At the pub, one of the senior members had called Harold 'Happy', and I wondered what that was about. I knew he was always joking about things, so that must have been it. *Anyhow it was a good nickname,* I thought. I had certainly heard worse, like dickhead, cement head, stinker. Yes, Happy is definitely a good one. I didn't remember anything after that until a banging noise coming from downstairs woke me up.

I looked around the bunk room, and there were quite a lot of beds with bodies in them. They must have come in through the night. A lot of yawning was going on, and a lot of naked bodies walking around, putting their bathers on and heading downstairs. I could smell sausages.

We went downstairs as a group and joined the line-up for brekkie. Bugsy Barron, the clubhouse director, was taking the money from all of the members as they filed past and ticked them off the list as paid. I couldn't help but wonder why Bugsy was called Bugsy until I saw him smile. He had a big set of white teeth, just like a rabbit. I had started to read some of the comic books that were lying around the clubhouse, and Bugs Bunny was a key character in some of the comics. I guess Bugsy was a fitting nickname. Just about everybody in the club had a nickname. I hadn't met Dirty Dirston yet, but I had heard some rumours about his reputation as a senior member of the club. He was a man to give a wide berth to. People said, 'Never find yourself in a situation where you are alone with him. He has been known to take things to the next level with the hardening up of young juniors just joining the club.' Why, I didn't quite get.

I was next in line, and a big plate of bangers and mash was passed to me. I found a seat at the end of the long table. There would have been about thirty of us all, talking and carrying on. Harold stood up and addressed the group as Vice-Captain. The club Captain had not made it down from Brisbane yet. Harold quickly introduced us three to the other members. I sat back down and had a quick look under my mash, just in case Jack the cook had put a cockroach or two under it. All was fine. The next thing I knew was I felt an excruciating pain in the middle of my back. I jumped up and the whole bunch were laughing and carrying on. I did not know the rule about slouching at the table, and Harold had not told me. An older man was standing behind me with a big grin on his face. It was Dirty Dirston.

'What the fuck did you do that for?' I said.

'You were slouching over your meal; that is disrespectful to old Jack, the cook.'

A penny had been thrown into the middle of my bare back by Dirty Dirston. He called out, 'Heads!'

Sure enough, Noel had a look at the mark it left and confirmed that it was a head mark on my back. My posture at the dinner table from then on improved. I sat back down, a bit embarrassed, and checked again for cockies under my mash. Then I did what Harold had said—kept my head down. Didn't want any trouble.

'Okay, you three new boys, you are on wash up.'

'No problem,' I said. *Seems like we are going to have to work our way in here*, I thought. These old blokes all looked pretty tough and were as thick as thieves.

Breakfast was memorable, to say the least, but the food was excellent. The wash-up was a big job and old Jack was really picky about his pots and pans. They had to be spotless, and they were by the time we had finished. Old Harry, the chief instructor who had timed us at Davies Park last week, came into the kitchen.

'Had a bit of skit from one of the seniors, yes?'

I said, 'Dirty Dirston.'

'Well, you'll learn in time. It is you young juniors against them. When you boys blend in with the other juniors, you will survive together.'

Crikey, I am thinking, *sharks, old blokes with an axe to grind, what next?*

'Now, boys, we are going to start our training for our bronze medallion this morning. I want you to meet me in front of the clubhouse on the grass in half an hour in your bathers and a towel. Do you have a hat?' None of us had one. 'Okay, go to the first aid room and find the big jar of white zinc. Apply that to your nose and lips for sunburn.' I had noticed all of the other boys had it on and didn't understand what it was for.

We were assembled on the grass and old Harry explained that a surf race was about to start and we were to take part in it. He handed each of us a green skullcap with gold and white stripes running from front to back, explaining that these were the Tugun colours. 'You keep your caps for both training, patrol and competition at surf carnivals. Now put them on and tie them off like this under your chin. Not a knot, but a bow, so that you can easily undo it at the end of a training session. Now as you know, I am the chief instructor of the club and my duty is to ensure that you get the correct training required to save a person's life from drowning in the ocean. A very serious responsibility, both in recovering a patient and resuscitating them using your first aid training. When the wind blows from the northeast here at Tugun, a creature called a bluebottle gets blown in from the outer ocean. It has long stinging tentacles that sting you and they really do give you some curry if you get stung.'

There is another one, I thought, *sharks, old blokes, now blue bottles; shit, I won't be game to go in the water.*

'Today, the wind is blowing from the south, so no bluebottles,' said Harry. 'The surf race is about to start, so go down and get in line with the rest of them, and Happy will give you the drill on how to swim in the surf race.'

Happy had sent a man on a surf ski out to drop a floating buoy. The idea was for us all to swim as hard as we could out and around the can, then back to the beach and run out of the water and sit down in the order we finished.

'I will take down your placings for the club's surf race champion of the year. Okay, remember, every now and then put your head out of the water as you swim so that you can see the can that you have to swim around. Try to catch a wave back to the beach once you have got yourself around the can. All got it?'

The other boys were on their marks and looking very serious; ready, go, and on that we all ran down, wading into deeper water so that we could start swimming. Some boys were jumping off the sand and diving forward, going underwater then diving out of the water and going under and springing themselves forward until they were in deep enough. They were a long way in front of us, and I put what they were doing to memory. *Wow, this is no cakewalk, I must say.* I had been hit by really powerful waves and kept getting driven backward. Eventually, I worked out a few tricks. By diving under the waves and letting them go over my head, I was clear of the beach, heading toward the floating can. I could see it when I lifted my head out of the water. There was a lot of kicking and pushing going on, but I got around the can and was on my way back to the beach. As I got closer, a wave came up behind me. *What do I do now?* I put my head down and swam as fast as I could, hoping it would drive me onto the beach. Well, next thing I was on my first wave. I had no idea what I was doing, so I just kept swimming as hard as I could. Suddenly, I felt sand under me, so I jumped up and started running as hard as I could up to the finish line.

'Sit down,' old Harry said, and he yelled out 'twelve' as I sat down, or should I say lay down. I was almost sick from exhaustion. Twelve was pretty good, especially when I had no idea what to do. Happy came third, and he was first to congratulate me. Brian and Noel were not far behind me. Harry had taken on a bit too much saltwater and had a bit of a vomit; you guessed it, sausages and mash, except the bangers and mash didn't look anything like the ones that had been served up to him at breakfast.

Well, I thought, *if this is Tugun Surf Club life, bring it on.*

Chapter 6
Roy and Judith

It was Monday morning, six o'clock. Billy Cummings and I were standing in the office of Chooka Lewis. I was feeling a bit sun-burned and stiff from all of the beach activities of the weekend, but I would be okay. This was my big day. Chooka, the head foreman, was talking to a couple of qualified butchers about today's slaughter tally. I heard one of them agree that four hundred and eighty-two was achievable.

It was going to be a hot, steamy December day, but with Christmas coming up, all the workers knew that every day counted to get the volume of cattle on the hook and into the cold rooms. Looking after any cattle over the ten-day Christmas break was not only expensive but also inhumane in the heat of a bare dirt holding yard for ten days, waiting for the inevitable. The two butchers excused themselves and left us with Chooka.

'Well, boys, day one. I have spoken to your old boss Ferpo Neuman down at the boning room about you, and he speaks highly of both of you.'

As Chooka talked, he went over to his desk, slid open a large wooden drawer under his desk, and selected four new, curved skinning knives and two long sharpening steels with two sharpening stones.

'Treat these pieces well; sharpen them every night, and they will serve you well,' he said. 'They have been sharpened and hollow-ground to keep the edge that you will need to do all of the tasks that you are going to be taught by your respective highly-skilled butchers. Roy, I have assigned you to Bobby Rylance, and you Bill are with Harry Irons. They are both good teachers, and I know that you will be well taught by both of them. Listen to them and don't try and do things that you are not up to. The art of skinning cattle is a very skilful trade. The skinned hide you are working on is a valuable part of the animal, and holes in the hide from not getting it right are a definite no-no. Got it?'

'Yes,' we said.

'Now it is time for you to take your place on the kill floor. Come with me, and I will introduce you to your respective teachers.'

Bill and I were dressed in our blue flannel, sleeveless, button-up shirts and string-tied navy blue shorts. No shoes, of course; the kill floor was always awash with water and blood.

As we were introduced and shook hands, Bobby moved me out of the way of the winchman who was delivering our first head to be processed.

'Come on, Roy, let's get into it. The quicker we go, the quicker we can get out of this hellhole.'

'Okay, Bobby.'

'Now Roy, you watch me as I do the first one and pass me the tools as I ask for them, so we can carry out each stage of getting this one to the saw.'

'Okay,' I yelled.

'Don't yell, Roy. We go steady and quietly, no panic.'

Okay, yes, Bobby.'

I was a bit nervous, which I guess was understandable.

'The steps of how we do this don't change,' Bobby said. 'These poor devils all have the same bits and pieces—four legs, one head, one tail, a gut and of course, one skin. We start with legging. The trick is getting the other bits off as quickly as possible, okay?'

I looked to the end of the kill floor, where I could see the knockers swinging their sledgehammers, bludgeoning each of the cattle, one at a time, until the animal was unconscious. Then the side of the knocking box would open up, and the animal would be winched up unconscious and hung on a rail system high above the kill floor. Next, a man in a yellow raincoat would slit the throats of each animal over the blood drain. As he slit the throat, a downpour of fresh blood would cover the 'sticker', as he was called. The animal was now dead and waiting for us to do our job. Bobby was calling on me to pass various tools to do certain things, and about half an hour later, our first one was back up, hanging on the rail, on its way to be vertically sawn in half. 'Well,' Bobby said, 'second verse the same as the first, Roy.' And we were into our second victim.

I got a go at legging—easy once you have done your first couple. I watched Bobby skinning and gave it a go. I got a bit tangled up but started to feel the flow of the blade of my shiny, round-shaped skinning knife. I could see Bill Cummings over the other side, going hard.

'My back is killing me, Bobby,' I said.

'Your back will get stronger, Roy, as you become more experienced.'

The horn blew, and it was smoko. *Shit, this is no cakewalk.* Half an hour later, we were going hard again. Lunch was in two hours, and the pace had picked up rather than slowed down. I was now doing more to pull my weight, and Bobby was a great patient teacher. I would be by his side for the next six months, then I would be classed as a butcher grade one, and my pay rate would be four times what I was on at the moment. This was a great incentive to become fully qualified.

It was Thursday arvo and I was standing in line, waiting for my turn at the payroll window.

'Hello, young Roy, I see you have stepped up around here.'

'Yes,' I said, 'trainee butcher.'

'Well, the management only put their trust in young men that they know will turn up each day and give their best. Mr O'Boyle gave your appointment his personal approval. Well done, Roy.'

Jim handed me my pay packet; wow, six pounds twelve shillings. I was very happy about my pay rise and would be able to pay Mum and Dad a bit more toward running the house. Onto my bicycle and into Burt Spenser's barbershop on the way home. I was going away to the surf club for another weekend, and some of us junior members were planning a night out at the beach house at Coolangatta where lots of girls went and danced. I didn't know about the dance bit, but the girls bit sounded okay.

I was third in line at the barber. Old Burt the barber was doing his usual thing, short back and sides. After he finished each customer, he took the two shillings, disappeared behind a curtain, and you could hear the sound of a bottle top being removed and then a pause. I was hoping that Burt hadn't had too many customers. I was sure the quality of his haircuts would vary based on how many times he had been behind the curtain. *Oh well, what could go wrong with short back and sides?* If you asked Burt for anything fancy, he would tell you to fuck off and go into those fancy barbers in town.

I was up in the chair when Burt returned from a session behind the curtain. *Here we go*, I thought. *Mum can tidy things up a bit if necessary*, although I did detect a bit of a shake in Burt's hands as he stepped up to the chair to start cutting my hair. *Lucky I have two ears*, I thought.

He asked lots of questions, like, 'How is your dad?' and 'What are you up to?' I said that Dad was not well because his lungs were letting him down and that I had joined the Tugun Surf Club.

'Give your Dad my best,' he said.

'I will.'

Burt said that his son Trevor was selling his Norton motorbike. If I was interested, it was out the back of the shop. I had told him that I was thinking about buying a motorbike. I was on the lookout for a good deal even though I wasn't old enough to get my licence yet.

'Well,' he said, 'it has been looked after and goes like a shower of shit.'

'I'll have a look at it after you finish my haircut if that's okay.'

'Yes,' Burt said.

I could sense a bit of a lift in Burt's hand strokes with the scissors. He must have been getting a commission from his son if he was to sell the bike.

Then came the tricky part with my haircut, the razor shave to the back of my neck. Burt's shaking had intensified. I didn't know whether the shaking was from the need of another beer or from too many trips behind the curtain. He seemed confident; it was just the shaking with a razor that was the scary part. *Oh well, still got two ears,* I thought. He brushed my collar off with his little brush. For some reason, he would hold a mirror up behind my head so that I could see his handiwork.

'Yes,' I said. 'That's great, Burt.'

I was out of the chair, handed over my two shillings, and walked out to the back of the shop in the direction of Trevor's Norton motorbike. It was covered by an old blanket. When I pulled the blanket off, there it was—immaculate, not a mark on it.

'You can start it if you like,' said Burt. I threw my right leg over and turned the key, gave it a kick, and the bike came to life. It had a softer tone than Barry's Norton and no sidecar. But I did not have a licence yet. I turned the key off, and all was quiet.

'Well, what do you think, Roy?'

'Well, I love it. How much is he asking?'

'One hundred and seventy-five pounds.'

Shit that is a lot of money, I was thinking. I had two hundred and thirty saved up and I had a better pay coming in. So I decided to ask my mate Barry to come over and have a ride to make sure there were no problems with the bike. I was beside myself with the possibility of being able to just get on and go wherever I pleased.

I explained to Burt that I was going swimming training at Davies Park that arvo, and I would get a mate to come over and take it for a ride. Burt was quick to jump in and said that his son would be home shortly so he could double me to the pool. Burt was a very good salesman. I think he was wasting his time as a barber. Sales in motorcycles would have been a better option!

I was hooked, and Burt hadn't had to get out of first gear with his sales pitch.

'Okay, are you sure?'

'Yes, it will be fine. Trevor is buying a new car, and he needs the money.'

I was thinking that getting Trevor to take me to the pool was a good idea. Barry was a tough nut, and he would be able to talk Trevor around to a lower price. I would go home and get my gear ready for Trevor to pick me up.

I had only just arrived at home when I heard Trevor powering up our street. I was telling Dad about my idea, and Dad was excited for me. As the bike pulled up, I ran down the front stairs. Trevor asked me if I wanted to drive, but I told him that I didn't have a licence. He explained that he could be my instructor because he had a licence. That made sense, so I got on, with Trev on the back. 'Okay,' Trev explained, 'the gears. One down, four up; the gear shift is on your left foot, and the brake is that lever on your right.'

'Okay,' I said. 'Barry, my mate, has the very same bike, and I have watched him carefully. I just haven't actually ridden it yet.'

'Okay Roy, squeeze the clutch and with your left foot drop her into first gear and accelerate a bit. Yes, that's good.'

We were moving.

'Okay Roy, off the accelerator and up two clicks with your left foot. Now, accelerate away. Okay Roy, pull her up at the end of the street and put both your feet on the ground. Left foot down, three clicks into first gear, accelerate and let out the clutch.'

Wow, I got it.

'Okay Roy, let's pick up the pace a bit and get her into top gear. You are going well Roy. Listen to the engine; it will tell you when to either change up or down by the revs it requires.'

I felt good. The trip to swimming was slow, but for my first trip, I thought I did well. I pulled up right outside the pool gate and gave the Norton a little rev spurt to show off a bit. I saw Barry's sidecar Norton parked across the road, and I explained to Trevor that Barry was here and that Barry would have a look at the bike after we finished training. Trevor said he would go down to the Coronation Pub and have a few beers while we trained. I thought that was a good idea; maybe a few beers might take the sting out of his bargaining power. Barry would know how to negotiate. The only downside was that if Trevor got the shits with Barry's negotiation, I would be sitting on the back of his Norton all the way back to Cannon Hill.

We trained hard with Mr Flemming, finishing off with a relay. I was the last leg for our team, and Barry and I hit the water at the same time for the last lap. I got a good dive and kept my head down for the first six strokes, getting half a body length lead on Barry. Up to twenty-five yards, and Barry was up with me. I gave it my all to stay with him. Then he was slightly in front of me. With six strokes to go, I put my head down and went hard. Bang, we both hit the wall.

'Too close to call, dead heat,' was the call from Mr Flemming.

We were both stuffed, and Barry gave me a little smile, then we both had a glancing look at each other and knew that I had taken my swimming to the next level. A good handshake and it was down to business.

'Now Barry, would you please have a look at the Norton that I am thinking of buying?'

'Oh,' he said. 'What is it?'

'Well, it is the same model as yours, but no sidecar.'

'Let me get dry and dressed, and I'll take it for a ride. How much is he asking?'

'One hundred and fifty quid.'

'Fuck, it will want to be good.'

'That's what I thought. If it's any good, maybe you could talk him down a bit, say to one hundred and twenty quid or so.'

'Okay, let's have a look.'

'Barry, this is Trevor.'

They eyeballed each other and shook hands.

'Hello mate. How many miles has your bike done?'

'Twenty-three thousand.'

'That is a lot of miles.'

'You can take it for a ride if you wish,' said Trevor.

'Well, I will, but while I am away, I want you to be thinking about the price you are asking. I think it is only worth one hundred and twenty quid, but I'll take it for a ride and give you my opinion.'

'Okay, yes, okay.'

Barry jumped on and gave the Norton a kick, revved the hell out of it and took off full bore. Trevor looked a bit concerned, but it was too late to worry about anything. Barry was gone, and both Trevor and I hoped that he would be back. It was late and getting darker by the minute. Five minutes later, Barry was back. As he pulled up, I was keen to know his opinion of the bike.

'Well, Trevor, the brakes are stuffed, and she needs a service. Other than that, she appears okay. What about a hundred and twenty pounds?'

Trevor nodded, and we shook hands at one hundred and twenty pounds.

'I'll meet you at Morningside Police Station after work tomorrow, and we can settle it there, both the money and the change of ownership.'

'Deal.'

'Thanks, Barry,' I said. 'Trevor, I'll let you drive home as it's getting dark, and I would not be confident.'

'No problems, Roy.'

'See you tomorrow, Barry,' I said.

'Yes, Roy, you will.'

Off we all went into the darkness.

Up the front steps at home and things were very different. Mum was crying, and Harold, Ernie, and Rita were also in tears.

'What's happened?' I called.

Harold stood close to me and told me in a quiet voice that Dad had died about two hours ago.

'What happened?' I exclaimed.

'Well, we think he had a heart attack and fell down the back stairs.'

'What, is he *dead*?'

'Yes,' said Harold.

'Where is he?'

'The ambulance took his body to the hospital.'

Mum was sobbing uncontrollably, and I was now in tears. Ernie stepped forward and hugged Mum. As the eldest, he would take care of all of the arrangements to get Dad's body organised and talk us all through the funeral arrangements over the next couple of days.

I would put the bike on hold. The funeral would be an expense to the family, and we would all want to give Dad the farewell he deserved. The army would have to be contacted so that they could get involved in a military send-off.

I went to the fridge and pulled out three beers. I asked Rita if she wanted one, but she didn't. She went to the kitchen and put on the jug to make Mum and herself a cup of tea.

The mood in the room was unforgettable. Dad was gone; my feelings for him were pouring out of me. He was my life, he was my everything. I didn't do anything without thinking about his opinion. He was a wonderful father, and he shared himself evenly through the family. I would always hold him close to my heart, and I would surround Mum with support as I know the rest of us would.

Ernie was going to try and find my other brother Tom to give him the news, and of course anybody else close to us. None of us were hungry, so we all said good night. We were going to try and get some sleep, but of course, that was impossible. Harold and I got into bed together, head to toe. He was still sobbing, and I was just in shock. Rita took Mum off to bed, and I am sure that she would have hugged Mum through the night.

The next morning, the alarm went off, and we were all in the kitchen.

'Rita, can you stay with Mum today?'

'Yes I can, Ernie. You and Harold go to work, Roy. No use us all moping around feeling glum.'

Five days until Christmas. *Not much to celebrate,* I thought, so I got on my bicycle and peddled my way to work. As I took my position on the kill floor with Bobby, he put his hand out and gave me a wonderful look.

'Thanks, Bobby; how did you know?'

'Bad news travels fast,' he replied.

I was a bit teary, but as our first head arrived, I decided to get on with it. That is what Dad would have wanted.

I was getting pretty good at skinning. Of course, I didn't get to sharpen my knives last night. Bobby had a spare one, and he lent it to me to get me through the day. I would work on my knives tonight. All through the day, some of my mates would come up and give me a handshake. At lunch, Chooka Lewis got up and spoke about Dad's passing and elaborated on Dad's war commitment to digging forward trenches in the dark. 'A brave, brave man and a great father' were his key words, which for me was a special thing. Despite Chooka's hard outside casing, a good soft heart came out in his speech. I thanked everybody for their thoughts on behalf of my family.

Back into it. It was payday. I collected my pay and was grateful to find an extra ten pounds—a gift from management to the family. That was also a great lift—to know that you are part of something and that deep inside this horrible place, we as human beings are surviving both physically and emotionally.

Mum was just about out on her feet. People had brought sandwiches and cake that would do for tea. I found a spot and sat down to prep my knives, ready for the next day. It would be an easier day with all the shock behind me.

Tuesday came, and it was time to say goodbye to Dad. Tom had arrived home in time. At ten am, we all got into Harold's and Ernie's cars and travelled to Hemmant Cemetery. Mum looked beautiful with a black chiffon hat borrowed from Mrs Johnson next door, and we all had hired black suits from the formal suit hire in town. Rita was particularly beautiful, dressed in a black suit and hat. As a family, we had done Dad proud. We all had jobs and enough money to give Dad a beautiful polished casket.

The whole neighbourhood turned up, and of course, four soldiers presented a guard of honour as a tribute to Dad's service. We were all doing our best to keep it all together. Ernie couldn't get through his speech about Dad, so Harold stepped forward and gave Ernie a bit of support. Then all of us kids stepped forward and Ernie got great strength from the family energy. I had never been to a funeral before. The grave was a desolate-looking place, and I had to try hard not to think too much about the finite part of what we were doing. I took comfort in Reverend Parson's kind words about everlasting life. I would make a better effort to attend church with Mum on Saturdays, now that Dad had left us. Dad loved hearing Mum singing hymns at home when she was doing the washing in the back yard.

Something came over me as I was standing in my position beside the grave. I thought of that little nurse at the burger joint at the Lighthouse Café. I could see her beautiful dark skin, her beautiful black hair and eyes. I actually felt that she was there beside me, just a beautiful smile saying, *All will be well, Roy, you will be okay. I am coming; we will be okay.* I even turned around; she felt so close, but she was not there.

As we were leaving the gravesite, I noticed Mr O'Boyle, the owner of the meatworks. He gave me a nod of respect and walked away. Again, a wonderful touch from someone important that cared about simple, local, honest and hardworking people.

I am important, and I will pursue and exhaust all avenues to become successful, whatever success means.

Life without Dad was tough, as to be expected, but together we strived for each other and of course gave Mum the support that she needed.

It was time to go back to Tugun. I had not been down the coast for what seemed a lifetime. A nice wave was rolling in, and we caught more than our share of body waves. On the way to the showers, I bumped into old Harry, the chief instructor who had timed us in our four hundred yard qualifying swim at Davies Park. He gave me his condolences and asked if my brother, Happy, was coming. I said that he was, and Harry gave a smile. 'It will be good to have you both back.'

'Thanks, Harry.'

'Are you going to the pub for dinner?'

I smiled back and asked if Dirty Dirston was down. Harry said that Dirty had started training for rugby league, and we wouldn't see much of the senior members of the surf club in the winter season. *That suits me*, I thought; *I will be able to relax a bit when we go to bed without being dragged out and bashed to 'improve our disposition'.*

The culture between the old members and the new members was that the beatings would continue until morale improved. The beatings bit was to ensure that the upcoming young members would not take a backward step in defending their traditional surf club spirit.

Funny thing, I would probably miss all of that. The senior members were all good-hearted men; they just had it in their heads that we younger lads had to be toughened up. I don't think any of them knew what I did for a living. I am sure that an hour or two on the beef kill floor would bring most of them to tears.

Great steak, salad and chips. The pub was almost full. Mr and Mrs Diamond, the pub owners, were on the turps, laughing and talking loudly. Betty held court to all and sundry—anything to keep the beer flowing, and flow it did. Butcher Feuerriegel and I had a couple of XXXXs, and at ten o'clock, the bell rang. As last drinks were ordered, a push and shove started just behind us. Everybody stepped back and let them have a go. One of the fighters was a lad called Donny, a member of the surf club. Donny was a heavy hitter and his opposition knew it. Donny's opposition put his hands up, and the fight was over. Donny was very drunk, and he said to his would-be opponent, 'You think you are tough,' and on that, Donny put the edge of his beer glass up to under his nose and tilted his head back. He then tipped the beer so that it ran down his nose into his throat, and when the glass was empty, Donny bit off a large piece of his glass and proceeded to grind the glass with his teeth until, to our horror, he swallowed the ground glass! If I hadn't seen it, I would not have believed it. Blood was oozing from Donny's mouth as Donny's would-be opponent was so shit-scared he walked away. *No good for me,* I thought, and grabbed Butcher on the shoulder to get out of there.

It was a beautiful moonlit night on our walk back to the clubhouse and a light southeast breeze. The sound of the surf coming from the beach helped me think of better things, away from losing Dad. 'The surf will be good in the morning,' I said, and Butcher agreed to get up early and have an early one.

Old Harry was going to give us both an accelerated bronze medallion training session in an effort to get our exam done before the end of the season. It would be tough going, but it would mean a head start for competing in surf lifesaving events at the start of next season. We were both totally committed to achieving that goal, so there would be some long days on the beach to get us ready for our bronze medallion examination before the end of April.

I will never forget that Saturday. We surfed and trained all day. It was about four o'clock and I was walking up the grassy bank in front of the clubhouse. As I got to the top, I raised my head and looked up and was completely taken by surprise. There she was, the little dark-skinned girl from the cafe. I walked over to her and said, 'Hello, are you the …' and before I could finish the sentence, she said, 'Yes Roy, it's me.'

My heart was thumping and I was almost in tears. 'How did you find me?'

'Well,' she said, 'I saw the Tugun surf lifesaving shirt you were wearing that morning at the Lighthouse, and I did some investigating, and here I am. I couldn't stop thinking about you.'

I told her my father died a couple of months ago, and she said that she knew. She had read it in the Births and Deaths column of the *Telegraph* newspaper. She was so sincere when she said that she was sorry for my loss. She said she was staying at the Surfmist Boarding House at Currumbin Beach and was getting the train back at four o'clock the next day. I asked if she wanted to go to the pictures at Currumbin, opposite the bird sanctuary.

'Yes, I would love to go to the pictures. What's on?'

'Doesn't matter; we have a lot to talk about. I'll meet you outside at seven o'clock.'

'Okay, it's a date.'

'Don't be late,' she said.

'I won't be late. Oh, what's your name?'

'Judith, Judith Morrow.'

'I'll see you then, Judith.'

'You too, Roy.'

Her smile was amazing, and I felt a warmth inside that I had never felt before. I was bursting with happiness.

I lined up for tea at the clubhouse: roast lamb and baked veg. I was first to finish and first into the shower. I borrowed some Californian

Poppy from Butcher to slick down my hair, donned a pair of good shorts and of course my Tugun shirt. Butcher was going to the dance at the Greenmount Guesthouse, and he was riding his Norton with his new leather jacket. He looked the ticket. I got him to double me over the hill to the old picture show that resembled an old army hut, and it probably was. Judith was standing out the front waiting, and I was on time. She offered her hand, and I took it. I bought two tickets for a comedy starring Bing Crosby. When the lights went out and the show started, I kept looking her way, still in disbelief of how she found me. The reflection from the screen made her cheeks glow a beautiful brown. I had a sick, nervous feeling in my stomach. I was in love.

Chapter 7
Life On the Beach

Now that I was seventeen, and finally had my licence, I dusted off the Norton. I used to scream down the Pacific Highway on my Norton, doing sixty miles an hour, Butcher Feuerriegel just behind me. He had the same bike, and every now and then, we would have a three-second moment of madness and open up the throttle to full bore. The speed rush was amazing, and an hour and a half later, we'd both be running down the beach like little kids.

I was old enough to try and achieve my bronze medallion and take my place in the surf club. On a beautiful Tugun beach morning, six o'clock, Butcher Feuerriegel and I were lined up with four other young lads from Currumbin Surf Club. They, like us, had been training for this day for the past few months. This was our attempt to qualify, the test for the right to become a surf lifesaver—not an easy feat. The reason for the combined clubs' attempt at the examination was that we were all wanting to compete in surf lifesaving events starting September the following year, and they, like us, were very excited to be going for it today.

We introduced ourselves, and I distinctly remember the name Marshall Kropp. He was tall, well-built, and from all reports could go hard in the pool. I guess the time would come next year when we'd be thrashing it out against each other. There would be various surf lifesaving events culminating at the end of the surf season with a national titles' competition to determine the best competitors.

The chief examiner had just been going through things with old Harry and the instructor from Currumbin, Henry Nix. Both Henry and Harry were very experienced and would not have put us lads forward unless they thought we were up to it today.

'Okay,' came the command, 'fall in boys.' And on command we lined up facing the water, tallest on the right down to shortest on the left, the shortest man being Butcher, and the tallest Kroppy. We were all in our best fitness possible, and today we would need to be on our toes to qualify. Today was a team test; if we failed, the six of us failed. Produce or perish, so to speak.

'Attention!' was the command from Mal McNeilly, the chief examiner, and we snapped to attention. *This is it,* I said to myself. *Mr McNeilly will determine if we are up to it.*

Mr McNeilly started off by thanking us all for the effort so far and then handed us over to old Harry and Henry to give the commands necessary to perform a mock surf rescue. First call, 'Positions', and on that we all marched into our pre-designated position. 'Lift reel!' On that, the middle four of us crouched, and together we lifted the surf reel up until we were fully back to our normal standing position. I was the designated belt man, it was my job to pull the surf line while swimming out to retrieve the pretend patient who was Kroppy.

Out of the corner of my eye, I caught the movement of a waving arm about two hundred yards to the north. There it was again. *Shit, that is somebody in trouble,* I thought. I quickly broke rank and called out to old Harry, pointing in the direction of the situation.

'Shit, Roy, you're right.' As it was early, there was no patrol on the beach. We were it. The next thing, Harry had us moving down the beach to the area where we saw the distress signal. We were all still in our positions ready to go.

Harry took over. 'Boys, this is not a mock rescue; this is the real thing. Let's keep calm. Okay, Roy, put the surf belt on and we will pay out the surf line until you get to the situation. Kroppy you get going and try to find the person in trouble.'

Kroppy was off and I was hot on his heels. We were both swimming hard and the boys on the beach gave me plenty of surf line so as not to slow down my progress. Kroppy yelled out to me, 'Over here Roy!' I was swimming as fast as I could. Pulling the surf line was a lot more difficult than swimming freely. The surf line was heavy, dragging in the sand as I swam. I could see that Kroppy had a swimmer rolled over on her back. She was a young female swimmer, motionless. 'Shit, okay Kroppy, get her over here to me and I will keep her head out of the water. Give a wave back to the beach.'

Seconds later I could feel the surf line pulling me back to the safety of the beach. I called out to Kroppy to swim back as fast as he could and tell the rescue crew on the beach the situation, and most importantly ring for an ambulance. 'Go hard, mate.'

On that, Kroppy took off. *Shit he is a strong swimmer,* I thought as he found his way back to the beach. Not much later I could feel the sand under my heels. *Well done boys!* They stopped pulling on the surf line and ran down to assist me to get to my feet with my young, rescued, unconscious patient.

Then, the four lads lifted the patient as they had been trained, and proceeded up the beach to dry sand, ready for her to be resuscitated. Old

Harry gave the call of resuscitation to Butcher who had shown a keen interest in resuscitation during training. Butcher knelt behind the head of the patient, and bent over to clear her mouth of some bile and vomit. Then Butcher started the lifesaving technique of chest compressions, known as the Sylvester Brosch technique. He was going well when the young girl's mother arrived at the scene, screaming and sobbing.

Shit this is serious, I thought.

Kroppy gave some support to the mother. A lot of people had gathered as well as the members of our surf club, then, thank God, a man, who had run from the southern end of the beach introduced himself as a doctor. He knelt down and gave Butcher a word of encouragement. 'Well done, son,' he said. 'I will try and find a pulse.' He reached over and took the unconscious patient by the right wrist, then moments later, the doctor told me to get ready to step in to Butcher's position in case Butcher got too tired to continue the resuscitation. 'She has a slight pulse,' the doctor called out.

Wow, I thought. 'Well done, mate,' I said to Butcher. He was in tears with emotion. The doctor gathered some towels to keep the patient warm and the resuscitation continued. 'Are you okay, Butch?' I said as he continued.

'Yes, Roy, I'm going okay. I'll finish what I started.'

I could hear the wail of the ambulance getting closer. As I looked down, I saw of the patient's leg move, and then she vomited. The doctor was there to clear her throat. 'Okay, son, you have done your bit. Well done. Let me in there.'

Butcher tried to stand up, but collapsed from exhaustion. The doctor was down talking quietly to the young swimmer and the mother had settled a bit. She told Kroppy that her name was Ruth. The two ambulance men ran down carrying a stretcher and a bag of medical bits and pieces. They were also pretty stuffed by the time they got to us. The doctor had helped the patient to a sitting position. She was still pretty shaken, but able to give us a little smile, then she was off on the stretcher.

Some of the other surf club members took a corner of the stretcher and carried her to the ambulance. The doctor and mother got in the ambulance and stayed with her to the Southport Hospital.

'Roy, Roy.' It was Judith. She was also upset by what had just happened, and in the confusion of the situation I had not noticed her. She put her arms around me and held me. 'Thank God you are okay. I thought you might have been attacked by a shark or something.' I reassured her that I was okay. The surf club lads now knew that Jude and I were together, and I was pleased as punch.

Old Harry was talking to Mr McNeilly, the chief examiner. Shortly after, we were all gathered around him on the beach. 'Well boys, I have never been more proud. This event today is why I am totally committed to the surf lifesaving movement. You lads, under extreme pressure, have saved the life of a young lady who will be forever grateful for our efforts here today. You have shown that you are certainly worthy of being called a surf lifesaver.'

He said to us all that he would be preparing the necessary paperwork to recognise what we had achieved. He told us we would not have to go any further with our examination. On that, some of the older club members heard the news and gave three cheers for the new life savers: 'Hip, hip hooray!' was the call, and 'Three cheers for the Currumbin boys, hip hip hooray!' I was sure that the six of us lads, no matter what surf club we represented, would always hold today as special.

'I think breakfast is in order,' said old Harry.

'Can Judith come to breakfast please Harry?'

'Of course she can.'

We held hands and found our way up to the grassy patch in front of the surf clubhouse. Harold was giving a reporter from the *Bulletin* newspaper a run-down of the incident. 'Hey boys, how about a photograph?' We all gathered together, the six of us and of course old Harry, Henry and Mr McNeilly, to have our photographs taken. Little did I know that the photograph would also make front page news of the *Brisbane Telegraph* newspaper.

Breakfast was bacon and eggs and a large pot of tea. Butcher was still in a bit of shock about what he had achieved in reviving the young swimmer, and was unusually quiet. *He'll be okay,* I thought.

We agreed that a paddle on our new surf ski built by my elder brother Ernie would be good. It was high tide and a perfect three to four foot wave was rolling in. 'Want to come, Jude ?' I asked.

'That would be fun Roy,' she said with a touch of excitement in her voice.

'Let's go.'

Judith was wearing her new two-piece bathers. I thought she looked the ticket, and I told her so. She was a little embarrassed, but we were on the surf ski and paddling out the back. Judith was sitting up the front and I was paddling. Hard to conceive that a couple of hours ago we were doing our best to save that young lady. I turned the ski around and waited for a small wave to start things rolling, then sure enough a nice three-footer stood up behind us. I paddled until we were on the wave. 'Stand up!' I yelled to Jude. She jumped up, and we rode the wave to the beach. 'Fantastic,' I called.

She jumped off and lost her balance. Jude was so excited that she was up and ready to go and catch another wave, so I spun the ski around and we were soon on our way out the back to catch another wave. My new ski was a credit to Ernie, who was a perfectionist. I could tell that by the way it handled the first wave. Then suddenly, I saw a bigger wave right out the back. I took a few more strokes with the paddle, spun the ski around and yelled to Jude to lie down and hang on. Next thing, we were on it and it was all happening. 'Slide back, Jude.' She did, just in time. The nose of the ski lifted a bit, broken white water all over us. I was doing everything I could to hold the ski straight, and we were very close to the last shore dump. I couldn't hold her, then straight down the mine we went. We were both thrown flying, into the broken wave. Poor Jude found her way to her feet, but as I stood up I could see that in the rolling fallout of going down the mine, her swim top had been pulled down and was displaying her breasts. I yelled out to her, but she fell over when she was hit by another wave. By now, she was aware of her situation and did the best she could to recover some dignity. We hugged each other and had a laugh. I had to do my best to not get too excited in the swimwear department. I grabbed my paddle and ski and started the long walk back to the club house. What a great way to spend a couple of hours.

As we walked, Jude carried my paddle. 'Happy Roy?' Judith said.

I answered, 'Never happier, love.'

Instead of Judith catching the train back to Brisbane that arvo, she agreed for me to give her a lift back on the Norton. She was on night shift at the Royal Brisbane Hospital, and we agreed to leave at three o'clock that arvo. In the meantime she would go back to her boarding house and get some sleep to prepare for her night shift. She gave me a kiss on the cheek and started walking north along the beach on her way back to Surfmist boarding house at Currumbin. I went back down to the beach, body surfing and giving a hand to manage the large crowd of swimmers that had gathered for a lunchtime swim. The water was as clear as crystal and the surf was getting even better with the tide starting to go out. The waves were a bit more challenging, with shallower water on the sandbanks.

Shit it was two o'clock. I would have a quick half-hour nap myself and then pack the bike and go and pick up Jude. On the dot of three, there she was, standing with her knapsack bag, and she looked great. I was a proud man to have Jude on the back of my Norton Commando. After a bit of sorting out with the gears, we were off on what was to become one of many weary trips back to Brisbane on a Sunday arvo after both having the time of our lives at Tugun.

From that day forward, Jude and I were a couple. We were happy to repeat the same Friday arvo to Sunday arvo ritual of sun, surf and sand. Sometimes we were both exhausted from trying to fit in all the beach activities along with late nights down at Coolangatta Beach House rock and roll dancing. On the ride home I would almost be asleep at the handlebars of the bike, but somehow we survived the next couple of surf seasons.

Our surf lifesaving season for the year came to an end and was winding down. It was now the end of April 1949. I was nineteen years of age; I was a fully-qualified butcher at the meatworks; I was in love with Judith. I was a very competitive surf swimmer and surf ski paddler; life was great.

I started swimming training closer to home, at the Manly Pool in Brisbane, with a new swim coach, Max Skinner. Max was a very experienced surf swimmer and was helpful in my surf swimming development. Swimming in the open ocean required far more skill than just swimming up and down the black lines on the bottom of a swimming pool. As winter found its way into our lives for yet another season, Judith became a part of my family.

Jude was coming over to celebrate her birthday at my home with my entire family. Mum and Jude got on extremely well. Mum was baking a special birthday cake to celebrate the occasion. My brothers and Rita would also have their partners there for the big night. Judith did not enjoy talking about her childhood, but she did let us know that she was born in 1930 in Normanton, a small town in the Gulf of Carpentaria, in far north Queensland. Her father was a bank manager with the Bank of New South Wales. She was taken from her family as a four-year-old and taken to an orphanage run by the Church Of England in another small country town called Leeton in central New South Wales. She became very uneasy talking about her family, so I didn't push it. I guessed as time went by, things might become clearer as to why she was taken away to a mission. For now, I loved her and couldn't wait to see her beaming smile. She obviously felt very secure in the family environment that I was fortunate to have.

We had a great birthday party and all got a bit drunk on too many beers, talking about our previous year on the beach, the exaggerated stories of sharks, waves, surf ski wave riding, and of course our motor vehicles. Poor old Mum hardly got a word in. Her church gatherings were a great part of her life and her beliefs were her life, other than us. When we all got together at home, things got a bit tight with the sleeping arrangements. Makeshift curtains were strung up around various parts of the house in order for us all to get some private time together. From time to time, laughter would break out when someone might not be able to keep their private, critical moments to themselves, and would end up in some out-of-control laughter, with the rest of us joining in. Breakfast together in the morning after was always kept to a respectful level. For Mum's sake, it was just not discussed.

We were all going to the Brisbane Show together. Us boys were rostered on to the surf lifesaving club's raffle ticket stand for three hours and then we were going to go and watch the judging of the live poultry entries for this year. Mr Johnson next door had several old English roosters entered and they were direct descendants of Dad's original chook run. So we are all keen to get involved, and of course Mr Johnson would be as pleased as punch to see us all. He never failed to take the mickey out of us boys, asking if we had been enjoying his backyard peaches that year. His prize rooster picked up first prize in its division, and we all gave Mr Johnson a rousing cheer. Then we were off to the Cattleman's Bar for a steak and a couple of beers, the girls enjoying a gin and squash. Mum had a sarsaparilla with ice and was starting to tire a bit from all the walking. She also had a little tear-up when Mr Johnson's roosters came back into our conversation over lunch. 'You know, Dad would be very proud of today's result, his roosters and all.' As usual, we all gave Mum the support she needed and decided to call it a day and catch a train back to Cannon Hill Station, where it was a short walk back to the house. The huff and puff of our steam train pulling out of the Exhibition Station on our way home gave me a chance to reflect back to my younger days of horses and dogs, all of whom had fallen by the wayside of life. Ginger, my horse, had died after an American soldier had borrowed her and accidently rode her into a barbed wire fence. She died an unfortunate death. And Choc, my kelpie dog, had also met an early passing after being bitten by a brown snake. I had managed to kill the snake with the back of a shovel, but poor old Choc went very quickly.

Jude was sitting beside me on the train and could sense my drifting thoughts. She put her hand in mine and gave a tight squeeze, and I quickly came back to us all in the cabin. I realised that everything was good and there would be other animals come into my life down the track.

However, there was trouble brewing at the meatworks. A new union delegate had taken over with the passing of our long-term leader, Mitch Stevens. It seemed that every time some small incident happened on the kill floor, it would be blown out of proportion and we would have a meeting and then go on strike, without pay. I did my best to keep a low profile. This time we were striking about the sandwiches that the fitters and turners got for working overtime not being up to scratch. This argument went on and on for a month, costing us workers a lot of money, for no reason to us. The straw that broke the camel's back was when it was decided to strike over the sandwiches again. Us hard workers were pissed off and several fist fights broke out. We were getting nowhere, when out of the blue a young butcher jumped up and demanded a vote of no confidence in the new union delegate. There was complete silence in the crib room. 'I second that,' another worker said. The new union delegate was stunned by the motion.

'That means we will have a vote.' Pieces of paper were passed around, and a secret vote was held, the count supervised by Chooka Lewis. The result was called as being carried. The ex-union delegate stood up and yelled obscenities as he stormed out of the meeting.

'Well boys, we need another union delegate.'

I suggested that the young butcher that moved the motion would be a good start. A cheer went up and young Warren the butcher was duly elected. Chooka agreed to give Warren any support that he needed from time to time.

'Let's get back to work,' young Warren yelled. 'I have some hungry mouths to feed back home.'

Soon after we were back in full swing, and life again fell into the steady and strong family direction.

Chapter 8

Roy and Jude Are Well Into Their Journey

Fast forward to September 1956. I was standing at the Hemmant Cemetery gravesite where Dad had been laid to rest ten years ago. This time, it was our dear mum who had fallen to the distance of time and life. Pneumonia had taken her.

This time at the gravesite, I was surrounded by all of my siblings, Mum and Dad's nine grandchildren, fellow parishioners, and neighbours—all of whom had attended to pay respect to Minnie, our mother. Reverend Parsons was still around to make sure that Mum's last wishes were carried out to the letter. Prior to Mum's passing, when Dad died, my sorrow was different. This time it was much tougher. Your mum is your mum, and there's the deep connection of her giving you life, while there was also an awareness of the sacrifices she made. She had a lifetime of giving throughout my life, and as I reflected and wept openly, I didn't remember telling Mum often enough how much I loved her. Those 'I love you Mum' words didn't come often enough in the day-to-day struggle of life. *They should have*, I thought. So I quietly blubbered to myself: 'Mum, I love you, and if there is everlasting life as Reverend Parsons insists, can you hear me Mum?'

I fell to my knees with sorrow. Jude and I had our three children—Allan, Janice, and Debora—gathered around us. The rest of my family were all in a similar state of emotion. The only reassuring thought was that Mum and Dad were side by side again. Dad would have been proud of the way that Mum had picked up the ball and given us kids the complete package of a family that she and Dad had strived to give us before his passing. And she gave our grandchildren the same values.

We made our way back to Mum's house at Muir Street. I took Jude and the kids up to Mum's backyard and our kids started to play. I looked at the wooden prop and wire clothesline stretched across the entire width of Mum's backyard that would never have the sheets and towels hanging on them again. When the clothesline was fully laden, it used to look quite magnificent, everything blowing around in a magical uncontrolled fashion. I remembered my dog Choc in his early days. He would swing off the ends of the dangling towels and Mum would chase him around and around the backyard with her straw broom. Choc took a few floggings from the broom, but he eventually got it and walked wide of the clothesline.

It was not long before all of Mum's grandkids were playing together in the backyard. You could only imagine the satisfaction that Dad hopefully would be having, knowing that the tent he had pitched on his two blocks of land here in Muir Street, bought for ten shillings each, way back in 1916, had eventuated in this assembly of wonderful children and grandchildren.

Jude and I had moved to forty-nine Keats Street in Cannon Hill, two streets behind Mum's place in Muir Street. It was a simple, low-set, three-bedroom weatherboard home in good condition. The house was on a thirty-two perch level block of land. Jude and I had paid twelve hundred pounds for it; how we raised that sort of money is beyond me. Our house was just perfect to bring up a family. Jude was now pregnant with our fourth child. We planned to be settled by the time the baby arrived, all going well.

A beautiful Sunday morning, and we were settled. I heard the engines of a small aeroplane circling in the direction of Porter's paddocks and then a splutter followed by a crunching noise. It could only have been the small aircraft crashing. I yelled out to Jude about what I had heard, and she suggested that I jump in the car and investigate. As I approached the gate to Porter's paddock, I could see a group of rescuers carrying an older Des Porter. I ran to offer help. Apparently, Des Porter was dropping some of his relative's ashes from the window of the family de Havilland bi-plane when he lost control and crash-landed into Doboy Creek. A passenger was trapped in the wreckage underwater, and Des was unconscious so unable to give any further hints as to what had happened. I ran down to the creek bank where the tail of the aircraft was sticking out of the water, but there were no signs of life. I quickly stripped down to my undershorts and jumped into the creek in an effort to try and find any survivors. The creek was a stinking boghole of waste from the bacon factory further down the creek. I could see a dead body floating inside the cabin, but it was impossible to get to it because the cabin was completely crushed. I swam back to the onlookers and told them the result of my investigation.

As a tow truck was on its way, I went to an adjoining caravan park and had a shower and clean-up. The new owner of the caravan park, called Peter, kindly gave me a towel and some soap. While I was there, I saw that Peter had built a swimming pool. So after I was smelling a bit better, I had a chat to him and asked if he would allow me to start teaching some of the local kids how to swim in his new pool. He was very keen for me to come back and have a further chat about the idea.

An ambulance had taken Des Porter to hospital. I hadn't seen much of Des since he had taken over the milk run after we left school and went our separate ways. I can still remember Des sitting in the milk cart up beside his Dad, and me on top of my horse Ginger pushing a mob of cattle to Samford twenty odd years ago. There was not much more I could do other than give the police sergeant a statement of what I had witnessed.

Back home, Jude had heard the news on the radio and was concerned about my safety. She had heard my name mentioned on the radio when they said that local surf lifesaver Roy Holland had swum to the aid of the trapped passenger but was not able to save him. I had another shower at home and used a cake of Solvol to scrub myself, adding some baby powder to improve the stench that had tainted my body from the stinking creek water. As I sat in the sun and enjoyed a cup of tea, I decided to mow the lawn. Mr Turner, who used to live up the road, had died. Mrs Turner was a great friend of Mum's, and her husband Bert had told her that I was to get his lawnmower. She was moving on and gave me Mr Turner's pride and joy, a Greens drum roller mower. I would long- and cross-mow to give a beautiful cut to our front lawn. It certainly did a beautiful job.

Barry Johns from Davies Park Swimming Pool had come back into my life. He was still living at Bulimba and had taken over the family soft drink factory. Every time he came to visit us, he would bring some bottles of soft drink. The kids loved them.

Jude was expecting our fourth child any day, and got good support from our neighbours, Mrs Underwood and Mrs Percy, who helped with the day to day running of the house while I continued at the meatworks.

'It's a boy!' was the call down the corridor of the Mater Hospital.

Another boy, I thought; two boys and two girls. All went well with the birth and Jude and I named him Stephen Roy Holland.

Barry Johns introduced us to another old dugout tidal quarry on the banks of the Brisbane River at Colmslie. For some reason, the locals called it Tahiti. The quarry had been a drydock during the war and was now a wonderful place for us to go swimming. Tahiti was an old excavated pit of porphyry sandstone which had been a source for the building of many fine old buildings in the eighteen hundreds. Here in Brisbane, the excavated stone was taken upriver by barge, unloaded at the New Farm wharf across the river, and then delivered to each building project where stonemasons would work their magic on the unfinished slabs of stone. It was important that the stone from one quarry was used for each building because of colour differences from each pit.

Barry was keen for me to get back into surf lifesaving, and I agreed to start swimming training again together at Tahiti. We both gave training a real big go. We cut up an old car tyre tube into two-inch-wide rings which we used to tie our ankles together so that we could not kick our legs. This technique improved our fitness, but with four kids and a mortgage, it was not possible and was unfair on Jude and the kids. And of course like so many things, once you have had a wonderful experience and try to get it back, it is never the same.

It was time for me to step up and think about the future. My surf club days were over. I was grateful for all of the memories that I had formed down at Tugun Surf Club. I would not have met Jude, the love of my life, if it was not for Tugun.

Jude had her hands full with four kids and I was going hard at the meatworks, so it was time. I had been thinking of the learn-to-swim opportunity ever since I spoke to Peter, the caravan park owner just near to where the small di Havilland had crashed. I had no idea what to say to Peter about my plans to start teaching swimming, but he was quite casual about the idea. He suggested that I should start off and see how it went for the first summer. That would give me a good start. The water in the pool was not filtered and was the colour of milk from the lime-based chemicals that Peter put into the pool on a daily basis. I didn't know anything about swimming pool water. *Oh well,* I thought, *I'll give it ago.*

Back at home, Jude and I started talking and planning how to start swimming lessons.

'Where do we start?'

Jude was very clever and was working on an advertisement in the local *Moreton Star* newspaper. 'How many kids in a class?'

'Well let's start with six, at two shillings a child, for a half-hour lesson.'

Jude set up the ad in the paper for the following Thursday, and we would see how we went. The ad read: 'Swimming lessons by Roy Holland, swim coach. Be at 49 Keats Street at 9 am this Saturday morning. Bring bathers, cap and towel. 2 shillings per lesson.'

I guess we'd know how we were going to go by about ten past nine next Saturday. I had an idea to build a swim platform out of the pool that would assist me to explain to each child how to kick their legs and the correct timing of turning their head, taking a breath, and blowing bubbles, getting ready to take the next breath. I had some plywood and timber and planned to start work on it after I got home from the meatworks the next day. The rest would sort itself out; if anyone turned up on Saturday.

Jude was assembling a booking sheet to keep tabs on the lessons. I was nervous about the chance that no one would turn up and failure was my greatest fear. I was in a bit of a tizz about what clothes to wear. I had a big straw hat and some black sunglasses that I had used on the beach at Tugun and decided to wear my Tugun surf lifesaving shirt and bathers to give the impression that I had some idea of how to swim. On Friday afternoon, I put the last touches of paint on the swim platform that I would take down early and set up. I had also cut some boards out of a sheet of plywood for students to use as kickboards, so they would learn how to kick their legs properly during their swimming lessons. God, I was nervous.

Jude brought out a cup of tea and a couple of Iced Vovo biscuits that she had managed to hide from the kids. 'Relax Roy; tomorrow will come soon enough.'

Next morning, the alarm went off, and I was up and at it.

'Jude, I'll have some breakfast when I get back from the pool, at about eight o'clock.'

'Okay, Roy, I 'll have some breakfast ready for you then.'

I went off to the pool, not knowing that the statement, 'I am going up to the pool' would become a huge part of our lives from this day forward. It was a beautiful day as I got the keys to the pool gate from Peter. I had offered to pay ten shillings up front, but he had refused it.

'Roy,' he said, 'I am one hundred per cent behind your idea. We'll talk money down the track. Get yourself home and see if anybody turns up.'

As I drove up Keats Street at eight-fifteen, I saw a couple of cars parked outside our house. As I got to the house, I was stunned to see four or five kids standing with their towels, waiting for some instruction on where we were going next. I parked my car in the driveway, got out, and was greeted by Jude. She had her lesson book going, taking the kids' names and their addresses and phone numbers if they had one. I was beside myself with excitement. Jude grabbed me by the arm and introduced me to a gathering of about fifteen kids. I thought I could get about ten kids in the

Plymouth sedan, including three in the boot. A parent offered to take the rest of the kids in her car. Her name was Peg Bailey, and she had two of her own kids. It was only a quarter to nine, and three more kids pulled up on their pushbikes. Mr Hallman from across the road had seen the ad in the newspaper and offered to back me up with lifts for some additional kids.

It got to nine o'clock, and Jude had collected two shillings from every child and parent.

'Okay, Jude, it's nine o'clock. Can you stay here? I'll take a load of kids and you can get parents with cars to follow me down to the Monte Carlo Caravan Park.'

Jude, as strong as ever, whispered to me, 'Well Roy, you have made your bed; you'll have to lie in it. Have a nice morning Mr Holland, swim coach.'

As we moved in convoy down Keats Street, the rest of the neighbours came out to see what was going on. *Future customers*, Jude was thinking.

When we arrived at the pool, Peter was standing at the gate with a smile that said it all. As I went through the gate, Peter gave me a pat on the back for support.

'Alright kids, strip down to your swimmers and stand around me.'

Amazingly, I counted twenty-two kids, all jumping around like they had ants in their pants.

'Okay, my name is Roy Holland and I am going to teach you to swim. If I tap you on the head, go and sit on the side of the pool. The others can sit on the benches and wait for their turn.'

My neighbour Mr Hallman did what he could to keep the next lesson quiet, but boys will be boys, laughing and giggling.

I got in the pool at the shallow end, where the water was up to my waist. 'Now slide in and hang on to the bar on the side of the pool. Turn around, face the side of the pool, and we will start kicking. Watch me to start with.' On that, I grabbed hold of the rail and started kicking my legs. 'One, two, three, four, five, six; keep counting and repeat the counting, one, two, three, four, five, six.'

Soon, the kids were full of splashing and giggling, and I was having trouble getting them to calm down. There were four boys and eight girls, and the average age of this group was about seven. I called out for everybody to understand that their parents had paid for them to learn how to swim, not giggle. That got them going even worse!

'Okay listen, the next boy to giggle will have to give all of the girls in the class a kiss on the cheek.' Well, that did the trick. No way was a boy going to go around and kiss every girl in the class, and nor was any girl going to have some strange boy kiss her on the cheek. Things took on a different tone; not a sound, just lots of kicking. Of course, the next group took the discipline more seriously. It was my first teaching tool, and I thought I would use it again.

The water was quite warm, but the lime was hard on the kids' eyes, so I developed a way of getting the kids to keep their heads down for six strokes eyes closed, stop and take a breath, and wait for the next child to do the same. This worked. Half an hour was long enough for a lesson as the water was burning their eyes by that point. I let the first class have a five minute play while I addressed my next lesson. While they played, I gathered the next group and briefed them on what was expected of them. No mention was made of the boys kissing the girls. Some parents that had gathered thought that my tactic to stop the kids from laughing and giggling was hilarious.

'Okay.' I blew the whistle that I had forgotten I had. 'First lesson out,' and away I went again.

It was obvious that six kids to a lesson was the way to go, but the differing levels of ability in the water was the problem. So next week, I would break the classes into groups of six. Jude would sort out the phone calls and give each student a time for their lesson next Saturday. I would do my best to remember who was who in the zoo.

Finally, my first Saturday morning was over. 'Let's get back to my home, and I will grade you and give you a time for your lesson next week.'

As I approached home again, the yelling and screaming in the back of my car was deafening. Three more cars were parked outside the house. I parked the car, and my first load of would-be swimming champions got out and stood in a group while Jude and I sorted out next week's lessons. 'Oh Roy, these other people have two kids each and want to attend next week.'

I explained to those parents that some kids were at a different level than others and that if they attended next week, I would grade them and they would advance at a faster rate in their own level, and not get embarrassed if they couldn't do what the other kids could do. The parents agreed. 'Thank you, Mr Holland,' they said.

'Jude will sort out a suitable time and I'll see you next Saturday.'

'Jude, I think I will put the head down for a quick nap.'

'Okay, Roy.'

On that, a knock on the front door with two more kids for next week. I couldn't sleep. 'How many kids now Jude?'

'Thirty, Roy. I think two more are coming with that last lot.'

'Wow,' I yelled back.

'Wow, alright,' Jude called back.

Then the numbers started to multiply in my head. I never had much of a brain for maths, but I was starting to get it. Two shillings at a time … as I lay on the bed contemplating the past four hours, I realised that this was what I wanted to do for the rest of my life, teaching kids to swim. I had never been comfortable working at the meatworks. The smell of death never left my skin, and the brutality of a day at the office took a lot of putting to one side, especially when you had kids. I found I was trying to juggle my emotions of the day in which I had witnessed all sorts of cruelty.

I fell asleep, and then Jude woke me with the news that she had booked another ten kids for next week.

'Jude,' I said, 'that is four pounds more a week to us.'

'Yes Roy, you start at eight am next Saturday and finish at eleven-thirty. I hope you can go the distance.'

'I will, Jude, I will.'

'Roy, I have calculated that if you can go till two o'clock on Saturday, you will earn around eight pounds. Your average wage at the meatworks is twenty pounds per week. Who knows, maybe we can make a real go of it.'

I hugged Jude and realised that Jude was the strong and clever person that I had fallen in love with. *All will be well,* I thought to myself.

A long, exhausting summer whizzed by. Our Holland Swim School was going well. However, because the extra volume of kids had risen to around eighty, the chemicals that Peter was putting in the pool without proper filtration was not good enough, and some of my pupils' parents were complaining. Jude and I had the opportunity to buy the house directly across the road. With our increased income, we managed to buy number fifty. The large, beautiful Queenslander was also on forty-eight perches of land. I was talking to Peg, the mother of two of my pupils, and I explained the problem I was having. She understood as her kids had been complaining of sore eyes. Peg looked at me and told me how much she believed in Jude and me and all the good that we were doing. 'Roy,' she said, 'what if I was to loan you seven hundred pounds?'

'What for Peg?'

'Well Roy, you have plenty of land with the new home, and Jude is pregnant again. You could build a swimming pool in your backyard. When you need the money, I will pay the bill and when it is finished, then you can start paying me back as it suits with no interest. How does that sound?'

'Peg are you sure?'

'Roy, I'm not rich. I inherited the money, and the person who left me the money asked that I do something good with it. I think that the number of kids' lives that you save by teaching them how to swim is the best thing I can do with the money.'

I was speechless. I couldn't wait to tell Jude. She'd had a surprise pregnancy and we now had two boys and three girls, adding our latest daughter, Cathy Leslie Holland. Jude was a fantastic mum. She just kept going. Jude had also been concerned about the pool water at Monte Carlo, so I hope she agreed.

I waited until the kids were all in bed, and then I dropped the bombshell about Peg's offer to loan us the money. There was no other way to say it than to give her the bottom line. 'We are going to build a swimming pool in our backyard, and we have the money.'

Jude was emotional at first but then started to think of what had to be done. 'If we make this happen, Roy, I guess this might seem an unusual question, but do you know how to build a swimming pool?'

'No, Jude, I don't, but Peg Bailey knows someone. His name is Bill Robinson and he builds swimming pools. Can you call him to come and have a look after work when it suits him? Peg will give you the telephone number.'

'Okay, Roy. I'll call him tomorrow. We have all winter to build the pool ready for the summer.'

From that point on, Jude and I became a team; a team that had a clear and precise plan of what was required. Our backyard was about a hundred feet wide so that the pool could run across it. I thought that the length of the pool should be about fifty-five feet; three laps for fifty yards. This would give me a fair idea of what time a pupil would do when they went to swim at the Valley Pool, which was fifty yards. The pool had to have a deep section to allow them to practise starting dives. I knew that you didn't want to be beaten in the dive in a race. You have to be first in the water and first to come up stroking as hard as you have been taught. Staying too long on the starting blocks doesn't win gold medals.

Mr Robinson was coming in the arvo to have a chat about our plans. I was so excited about our progress that I raced home as fast as I could. I saw a builder's truck parked in the driveway, with a sign on the side that said 'Robinson Bros. Pool Builders'. Jude and a tall, fit, middle-aged man were standing in the backyard where Mr Robinson had a large measuring tape.

'Roy, this is Bill Robinson.'

'Thanks for coming Bill.'

'So, Roy, what do you have in mind?'

'Well, I have no idea of how to build a pool, but I know what I need, so maybe we can start there.'

'Okay, I'll ask a few questions. First, how long do you want the pool to be?'

'Well I want three laps of it to be equal one lap of the Valley Baths.'

'Yes, that's achievable. How wide?'

'I want four lanes. That is about fifteen feet wide.'

'And the depth?'

'I want the pool to have two shallow ends at a depth of around three feet and at one end I want to have a deepened area for race starts. That area should taper from three feet to five feet.'

'Good, Roy. All of this is achievable. How much is your budget?'

'We have been loaned seven hundred pounds to get the pool built including a filter.'

I explained that I was teaching at a caravan park pool without filtration. 'It is too hard on the kids and unhealthy.'

'Yes.'

Bill agreed that there was certainly a need for learn-to-swim here in this part of Brisbane.

'Roy it will cost double that amount to build the pool you have described.'

My gut went tight and I was devastated at his news.

'But you look like a hard worker, and I am sure you have some basic skills. How about I manage the build for you? There would be no builder's profit, and you can pay all the bills. If you do exactly what I tell you to do, then the seven hundred will do the trick. You and Jude have a chat. I suggest that if we decide to go forward, Jude can do all of the paperwork and that will keep things under control financially.'

'Okay, Bill, we'll have a chat and call you with our decision. Do we have to get approval?'

'Yes,' Bill replied. 'I can organise that, and you pay the costs.'

'How long will the pool take to build, Bill?'

'We are entering the winter season, so if the weather is kind to us it will take about four months.'

'That time frame is good for us as we want to restart lessons at the beginning of September.'

I tried to control my emotions. 'Bill, can you have a look around and Jude and I will have a quick chat?'

'Okay, Roy. I can come back if it suits.'

'No, Bill. Just give us a few minutes.'

'Okay, Roy.'

'Jude this is our chance. This man is genuine, and he will get the pool built on time; the costs will be controlled by us, so I say let's go.'

'I'm with you, Roy, let's give it a go.'

I grabbed Jude and held her. 'Okay, let's get Bill underway.'

'Yes, yes, yes, yes,' said Jude.

'Well Bill, we want to go forward.'

Bill put out his hand. As I took it, Bill looked me in the eyes and said that he would not let us down and all would be well.

'Okay, the measurements are fifty-five feet long and fifteen feet wide, three feet to a deeper middle, say five feet, and back up to three feet at the other end, in the centre of your backyard.'

'Yes,' we agreed excitedly. On that, our latest baby Cathy was giving a bit of a cry and the other kids were starting to get a bit rowdy.

'They are hungry. I'll let you see Bill to his truck.'

'Okay.'

'I will need you to get a title plan showing where your house is located on your land: your bank will have the title deed. All you have to do is make a hand copy, and your bank manager will help you with those details.'

Jude explained that their bank manager brought his two girls to lessons.

'Perfect,' Bill said. 'Jude, can you call me and let me know when you have that drawing copy?'

'Yes I will Bill.'

'Roy, I will get the approval organised and we will plan to start on Monday the first of May 1960.'

'What are the first steps?'

'Well, we'll do a set-out and I will bring in my bulldozer and truck. We will mound all of the diggings down at the east end of the block, and I will load and get rid of the fill.

At 7 am on Monday the first of May, it was a perfect day to start digging. I had taken a sickie from work to do whatever Bill needed. A few weeks later, and word had got around the neighbourhood that it was time to pour the pool floor, but the catch was that the pouring had to be done all in one day to stop any cracking down the track. A small army of workers turned up the next Saturday morning to shovel and wheel the mixed concrete to the feet of Bill Robinson, where his men would rake and place the concrete into position. I had no idea that I had the support of so many parents. Several ladies made sandwiches and a big pot of hot tea. We were a well-oiled machine. The last barrow load was wheeled into position by mid-afternoon. I went down to the Tingalpa Hotel and bought two cartons of XXXX beer. I was not a drinker, as I had had the fags and grog belted out of me by some of the older members at the Tugun Surf Club. Back to the backyard, and the beer was appreciated by all.

Sooner than later, I was standing on my own in my own backyard with a huge pile of dirt at one end and a great big hole with a concrete slab at the bottom. *Shit,* I thought, *hope Bill turns up on Monday.* He would be starting to build the concrete block walls with his block layer tricky Ricky the bricky, as Bill called him

Upstairs, I was absolutely stuffed. Jude was up to her neck with excited kids. Young Allan, who was nine years old, had shovelled all day and had gone to bed, also totally stuffed.

'Well, Jude, we are going well.'

'It certainly looks like we know what we are doing don't you think Roy?' she said. 'I have all the confidence in the world in you Roy. You will make this happen, I know it.'

Hugs all round. In a couple of weeks I was going to start advertising in the newspaper for interested parents to enrol their kids in lessons starting Saturday September 1.

'That would give us time to see if you can leave the meat works.'

'Shit,' I said, 'leave the meatworks? Jude aren't we jumping the gun a bit?'

'No Roy, if we are to make a go of this then you need to be fresh, to deliver the best possible result for our paying customers. You may have to go back to the meatworks and get us through the winter.'

'Good plan Jude.'

From there on everything went to plan. On the first of September, I started the first lessons in my own pool with beautiful clear filtered water and four perfectly-marked black lines that were more for show at that point. I was booked out Saturday and Sunday and Jude had started to take names for a training squad. That would be held three afternoons a week after school.

Good idea, Jude, and all at two bob a lesson. Well done, Jude, well done.

Chapter 9
Living the Family Dream

It was 1963 and our swimming season was about to start. I would teach forty hours a week and the volume of kids coming to the pool had increased to around four hundred and fifty. As Jude had predicted, I went back to the meatworks for four months to top up the family financially. I guessed the return back to the meatworks was more of a revisit to give me my self-confidence a lift. I received a bit of rejection from some of the other workers who were still doing the same shitty work day in and day out without any possibility of a better offer coming their way. I was very glad to call it a day for me and the meatworks, thanks to Jude and her vision for our future. I had taken Allan, my eldest son, to work on the beef kill floor on the school holidays. Looking back that was a mistake as it was no place for an eleven year old boy. The misery never leaves you. I hoped Allan could find his way through it.

I had been getting things ready for the coming 1963 swimming season. Allan and I had built another dressing shed for girl learners and upgraded the boys' shed at the eastern end of the pool. We went back to scavenging for second-hand timber from the public rubbish dump down the road at Tingalpa, not far from the spot where Mr Porter the milkman had crashed his aeroplane. I also decided to repaint the inside of the pool and of course those dreaded four black lines.

We kicked off the season the following Saturday morning and I was well prepared for the long summer in front of us. I was particularly looking forward to seeing Jude sitting at the kitchen table, wading through a pile of coins and notes, ready to go to the bank. That gave our family the security that we had become accustomed to. Jude had found an accountant to sort out our tax at the end of each season. We were now a thriving business and had to pay our taxes and keep the business solid. *Beyond me*, I thought.

I always got a bit nervous in the lead up, and of course Jude had her hands full with running the house and taking bookings for lessons. Jude and I decided to start running training squads five days a week. This was due to the demand from pupils coming through after they had achieved their goal of being able to swim two laps of the pool without stopping. This gave me great satisfaction. More training squads would free up the pool and give more kids the opportunity to attend swimming lessons. Instead of having one training session per afternoon, we were planning to have a second squad for advanced swimmers that had come through the ranks and had shown further interest in becoming a champion swimmer.

All of my kids were now involved in either competitive club swimming or school swimming. The two younger kids, Stephen and Cathy, were showing signs of becoming good swimmers, especially Stephen. He and Cathy had been playing in our pool as three and five-year-olds. I hadn't had to give them any lessons. They dived, played tiggy, and swam with their heads down for as far as they could hold their breath. Stephen could swim over and back across the pool freestyle and all on one breath. Jude joked at the dinner table that Stephen had grown some fish gills and was maybe a dolphin.

'Good name,' I said.

'What do you mean Roy?'

'I mean Holland's Dolphins.'

'Yes Roy, that's it; we are now the Hollands Dolphins. How about a sign out the front?'

'Great idea.'

I planned to speak to one of our parents who was a signwriter.

'Great, oh and don't forget everyone, this Tuesday is the first club night for this year.'

'Okay, Mum,' the kids responded.

'Oh, Stephen, it's your first race in the twenty-five metre freestyle.'

Stephen's eyes lit up like a light bulb, and he gave me a big grin.

'Don't forget Stephen, every time your left hand enters the water, turn your head, take a breath, and don't forget to blow bubbles ready for your next breath.'

We were all excitedly gobbling down our dinner so that we could watch the news on our new television set. The kids were struggling with their greens, but managed, with a little bit of encouragement from Mum and the strap sitting beside her. Jude was a firm believer in eating everything on your plate. She had told me of her six years at the Church of England mission in Leeton after her mum had died when she was only four years old. You ate everything and cleared the table when you were finished.

The telephone was forever ringing confirming bookings for lessons and cancellations. Jude had a large piece of cardboard all marked up with each half-hour lesson, six kids to each lesson. She was well on top of her game with being organised. All I had to do was walk from one side of the pool as I finished a class and go to the other side where Jude would have the next set of kids sitting ready for me to start their lesson.

We all watched the news together. No need for a bath or pyjamas because we had been swimming all afternoon. *Good enough*, we all thought.

It was Tuesday arvo. Jude and I had got everything sorted after training and we were off to the swim club night at the Valley Pool, the headquarters for swimming here in Brisbane.

'Quick Roy, take Stephen down to report in for his first race.'

Stephen was in his bathers and jumping around with a nervous jig. We were behind the starting block at lane four when I noticed the starting blocks were half as tall as Stephen and I had to help him up on to the top.

'Okay Stephen. Just like I said: stand up straight and listen to the starter's instructions. The rest is up to you.'

'Take your mark, get set, and bang, off went the starter's pistol. When Stephen hit the water, he totally forgot everything I had said. He just took off and kept his head down almost the entire twenty-five metres, leaving the rest of the competitors completely for dead. I hoped that there was not a rule that insisted you had to take breaths! We just accepted that Stephen was able to do this and all move on.

Jude was at her usual spot near the finish line with two stop watches and the names of all of the Hollands Dolphins who were competing that night: distance, last time recorded, and this week's time, plus or minus in seconds. That kept me well informed as to who was improving and who was not. Jude and I would have plenty of things to talk about on the way home. Most of our kids would fall asleep in the car on the way home. After a long day around the pool, the pillow was a welcome end to the day.

Jude had heard of an old swim coach, Mr Joe Emerson, who was a very experienced freestyle coach. He was all about stroking in the water correctly. Jude and I thought it a good idea to send our eldest boy Allan to get some finer tips on his freestyle stroke. Allan could catch the tram from Balmoral and get off at the Valley Pool by eight each Saturday morning. Allan was a bit apprehensive, but Jude assured him that he would enjoy the break from swimming at our home pool. Allan's first trip on his own was a good experience, and although Mr Emerson was a bit of a crabby old bloke, Allan and he got on well. Meanwhile, Stephen was training in the big squad at home. He was a good listener and I was learning a lot from him although he did not know it. At this stage, he was six years old and seemed to be improving by the hour. He had developed a stroke that he could keep going for the entire training session and never whinged about how many laps had been set on the day. He was very competitive and hated anybody coming up beside him and maybe giving him a bit of a rev up with some short lived pace. Most times, if anybody passed him, Stephen would turn things around and wear him or her down. His times for fifty metres kept dropping every time he swam.

Jude and I knew we had a very special swimmer coming on. We would give him everything he needed to hopefully reach his full potential.

Hollands' Swim School was also growing at such a rate that Jude had bags of money stored all over the house. Sometimes I would wake up and say to Jude that I had a sore back from trying to sleep on all the bags of coins that were stashed under the bed. Jude would proudly say, 'Roy, winter is coming; no more meatworks, right?'

'Yes Jude.'

She would say, with a sense of pride, that it was a good problem to have.

The backyard pool was bursting at the seams with swimming kids and their parents, a hive of activity, and Jude always kept her cool, staying in front of any oncoming problems. Jude and I were so intent on giving value for money that when classes were underway on Saturday and Sundays, if I thought that a particular child was not up to the level to that of the others, I would say to Jude, 'Jude this little one needs to go back a couple of grades where she (or he) would get a better go.' The parents all accepted this and Jude would move the child into another class that better suited their standard. Of course all this was done on the large piece of cardboard that Jude would write up on Mondays ready for the next weekend's lessons. A well-oiled machine. And at this stage, it was just Jude and I, going hard, day in day out, with a common goal of teaching as many kids as possible and producing swimmers that both of us were proud of.

The 1963 season was coming to an end Jude and I had worked ourselves to a standstill. My voice was ready to throw in the towel and we were both ready for our winter break. The only swimming that would come into our lives in winter was Jude taking Allan out to a twenty-five metre heated pool at Aspley on the northern side of Brisbane. *Wow,* I thought, *a heated swimming pool; never heard of in Brisbane until now.*

Jude did not have a driving licence and she was at first a bit apprehensive about driving, but after a few lessons from a driving instructor, Jude got her licence and we bought a second car, a Morris Mini Minor. This gave Jude a huge lift in her own confidence, as she could go off and do the shopping and take our kids to and from other activities that the kids had all moved forward with. It was a great go forward for the family. Winter was also a great time for the family to catch up on normal things.

I bought a plywood twelve-foot dinghy with a three-horsepower Seagull outboard motor on the back. I was as pleased as punch. I gave the dinghy a coat or two of paint and did a bit of work on the boat trailer that came with it. The trailer was a bit ordinary; it had no mudguards or indicators, just a modest steel frame and two wheels, like something out of Roman times. It didn't matter, because there was a boat on it with an outboard; that was all that mattered, and a chance to sail the seven seas. I had heard of a place called the Hanlan Light out in the middle of Moreton Bay, that was renowned as a spot where masses of winter whiting could be caught. I spoke to Noel Galloway across the road who was a professional fisherman and crabber. He knew Moreton Bay like the back of his hand. He said that he would let me and Allan and Stephen follow him out into the bay in my boat and he would show me the ropes of how whiting fishing was done.

'You'll need a hand reel each and some bloodworms, that you dig up with a fork at low tide down at Wynnum, a bayside suburb not far from our home. If you like, I am going to go and dig some worms in a couple of hours when it will be low tide, perfect for digging worms.'

Great. I got the garden fork and the two boys. I thought that they would learn a lot from the experience. Two hours later, we were digging in gravelly mud with my four-pronged fork, capturing plenty of bloodworms. The two boys were getting right into it and were now covered in mud. But it didn't matter because the adventure was getting these worms for bait. Tomorrow we would head out into Moreton Bay in our mighty dinghy and catch some whiting for us all to eat.

Well, that was the plan. Either way, it was a great opportunity for the boys and myself to spend some 'boy time' together. I thanked Noel for his lesson in worm-digging and we agreed to meet at the boat ramp at Cleveland the next morning at 7 o'clock sharp.

'We'll be there,' I said.

Across the road, I could see that the fish and chip shop was still open. 'How about some hot chips boys?'

'Yeah!' was the call.

I ordered two bobs-worth of chips, and before long, the three of us were hoeing into a large pile of red-hot potato chips. *Life is good*, I thought as we drove back home to share our plan with Jude and the girls.

The break in our learn-to-swim life was certainly welcomed by all back home. Jude was busy with the dinner prep and Janice and Deb were practising some dance steps they had been learning. Everybody was on the hop. Cathy had started Irish dancing classes and was a natural. We were all jabbering about the fishing trip tomorrow … who was going to catch the most whiting.

We were at the boat ramp early. I launched the boat and got the boys to hold the bow while I took the trailer up to the carpark.

'Allan, don't let the boat touch the rocks on the side of the boat ramp.' I didn't want to put a hole in the dinghy. As I was walking back, I could hear Allan calling out, 'Dad the boat is filling up with water.' *Shit!* I ran over to investigate sure enough the dinghy was taking on water. A quick look at the back of the boat revealed that I had not put the bung in, so water was filling the boat rapidly.

'Shit, I forgot to get a bung. Allan, come down the back and put your thumb over the hole while I find something to plug it with. Don't take your thumb off until I get back.'

Allan did as he was told while I ran around and found a suitable piece of stick and a piece of paper that I could shape and jam into the bunghole. Fortunately, my neighbour Noel arrived and was quick to give me a bit of stick about no bung in the boat. I was so worked up I came a cropper on the boat ramp, taking a bit of skin off my bum. I was really pissed off with myself. Noel came to the rescue with a spare cork that he had stored away in his boat. By this time, I had lost all sense of what to do next.

'Okay, Roy, you hop in the boat and get the outboard started. Then I'll put the two boys into your boat.'

I hadn't thought to start the outboard before I left home, and all sorts of negative shit was going through my head: *Would the outboard start? Don't ding the propeller on the concrete boat ramp. Shit my bum is hurting. Keep going. These bloody whiting would want to be plentiful after all this. Here goes.*

I wrapped the starter cord around the flywheel of the motor. 'Okay, Roy, give the bloody thing a big pull.'

Woosh, I gave it everything I had, and as I did, I fell arse over tit backward, landing in the middle of the boat on my bum again. A loud *hooray* went out from a group of other locals that had gathered to watch the performance. The only good thing was that the bloody motor had kicked and started; the bad news was the outboard was in forward gear and was pushing the dinghy around and around in a tight circle up the concrete boat ramp. I struggled to sit up on the back seat of the dinghy and start to gather some dignity and control, disengaging the forward control lever on the outboard. All of this chaos brought spectators at the top of the ramp, laughing and cheering. My two boys had a look of terror on their faces—what could possibly go wrong next? Stephen was lowered reluctantly into the dinghy and Allan jumped up the front. 'Can't wait to catch those whiting,' Allan said excitedly. I tried to be positive but was running out of enthusiasm.

'I will wait for you out of the way, Noel.'

'Good idea, Roy.'

Noel was also chuckling to himself, laughing at what was to come next. Things settled down a bit and before long we were tailing Noel across the bay trying to put the events of the boat ramp behind us. Noel was pulling crab pots as we went. Sand crabs were plentiful at this time of the year and Noel knew all there was to know about catching sand crabs. He was pulling up his pots, or at least what we hoped were his pots, trying to outrun an opposition crabber. With a three-horsepower outboard, that scenario would end up in tears for us.

An hour later we were on the spot: Hanlan Light, which is still a major navigation light at the southern end of Moreton Bay near Peel Island. Peel Island was a designated leper colony run by the government of the day to isolate people with leprosy from the population in Queensland, but it was abandoned in 1959.

'Okay, Roy,' Noel yelled. 'Start fishing.'

I sorted the boys' lines out, first showing them how to put a piece of worm on each of their whiting hooks. 'Now boys, lower your hook and sinker over the side until it is on the bottom.' The two boys were excited that they were fishing. I had heard a saying about fishing years later: 'Fishing is not a matter of life and death; it is far more serious than that.' I still don't know what it is about fishing, but it certainly gets you hooked, excuse the pun.

'Shit!' Allan said. 'Dad I've got one.'

Next, Stephen was calling out, 'Dad I've got one too.'

I was trying to bait up my own line while the boys were pulling their fish into the boat. I hit the panic button again—my line was not even in the water yet! *Bugger*, I thought.

'Dad can you take mine off?'

Bugger.

Allan was older and had fished before so he was okay with unhooking his own fish.

'Put yours in the bucket, Allan,' I said. His line was back in the water before we knew it. I was sorting out Stephen's hooked fish when Allan called, 'I've got another one.'

Well I was beside myself, trying to get Stephen's fish off, and get my line in the water. Then sure enough, Stephen got another. I finally got my hook on the bottom, and I had a fish on. Halleluiah, the whiting were on the chew and were quality fish.

'How many are we going to catch, Dad?' said Stephen.

'We can keep fishing until we run out of bait.'

'Okay, Dad, great,' said Allan. 'Dad if this keeps up, we could fill the boat.'

'No we won't, boys.'

'Hey Dad, have we got plenty of petrol?'

I went quiet and, without trying to scare the boys, I carefully unscrewed the fuel tank lid to do a casual but calculating check on the level of petrol still left in the outboard tank. *Shit, just on half full.* Sort of took the shine off fishing a bit. All I kept thinking about was, *Will we make it home?*

The wind was gentle. 'Oh stuff it, let's keep fishing.'

Noel was nowhere to be seen but there were other boats around us; what could go wrong? Well, an hour later and another bucket full of fish and it was time to put the petrol issue to the test. The motor started first go, thank God. I lined up Cleveland Point and kept the boat in a direct line so as to use the minimum amount of fuel. *Please Lord,* I prayed to myself. I only prayed to the Lord when I was absolutely terrified, and this fuel thing was going to be close. The motor was purring beautifully as I stopped the boat and checked the fuel. Shit, about a third left. *Going to be close, going to be very close,* rolling around in my head.

Then Cleveland Point, our destination, was starting to come into view. We were still going. Under my breath, I vowed to never leave the boat ramp without extra fuel and a spare cork for a bung. Closer and closer with every minute, we came around the point. I was trying to keep cool and not let the boys know the real situation. We were approaching the boat ramp when the outboard gave a puff and a splutter, the boat gliding to the ramp. We were out of petrol, but safe. I didn't let on to the boys. They would tell Jude and that would not be good.

Jude and the girls all came out to welcome us brave fisherman home. On the way home, I had briefed the two boys on keeping the events at the boat ramp between us. I explained that their mum would only get worried the next time we went fishing in the bay. We all agreed to keep our secret. Then, at the same time, we all started laughing our heads off as we remembered the whole boat launching event. Quietly, I again vowed to myself to be more organised, now that I knew the procedure of going whiting fishing in the bay.

I reversed the boat up and onto the driveway. The two boys got into the boat and proudly passed the two buckets of fish to me. 'Let's take them up into the kitchen and we can all scale and gut the fish. I'll fillet them as you all scale and clean.'

The kitchen was awash with 110 beautiful fresh whiting, and we were having crumbed whiting and chips for dinner.

Jude excitedly called out, 'I'll make you a cuppa, Roy, and you boys have earned a soft drink from the pool fridge. I'll get them for you.'

'Thanks Mum.'

'What about us girls, Mum?'

'Well, okay, we can all have a cold soft drink.'

On that, the two boys and I started the job of turning two buckets of whole whiting into 220 fillets of fresh whiting. 'Yummo,' I said and the boys chimed in, 'Yummo!'

The rest of winter was a great family year, but we all knew the inevitable was coming—summer, and sooner or later, hundreds of kids and their parents would descend on our home and Jude and I would continue on with our business dream.

Chapter 10
Carina Pool

It was the winter and Stephen was heading towards becoming the fastest long distance swimmer the world had ever seen. Jude and I had befriended a new coach on the block called Laurie Lawrence. Jude and I had agreed to close down the business at Keats Street in Cannon Hill and move to a swimming centre at Carina, a couple of suburbs away. Our business at home had outgrown itself and Stephen's career needed a fifty-metre heated pool. The Carina swimming complex consisted of three pools: fifty-metre, twenty-five metre, and a wading pool. It also had two squash courts and a residence onsite. The business had the potential to be expanded and a meagre wage came with the job. The complex was owned by the Camp Hill Carina Welfare Association, and was headed up by Brisbane's former Lord Mayor, Clem Jones.

At the time, the deal sounded good, but as time went on, the harder Jude and I worked, the less money we actually made. The two squash courts were later brought under our responsibility and they required a huge number of hours. Jude would base herself over at the squash courts at night, and I would prepare meals and take them over to her. She usually found her way home most nights between ten and ten-thirty. Jude's day consisted of a 5 am start, making sure that breakfast was organised for everybody, and the rest of the day was a mix of training squads, swim schools, learn-to-swim classes and of course those bloody squash courts. The onsite house was home for the seven of us. Then, our eldest son Allan had a major hiccup and he had to move in with his two kids, Troy and Shona. So with Allan and the two little ones, there were nine of us. The bedrooms had two double bunks. Amazing times, but the family stayed strong.

Stephen was the family focus as he was giving his swimming enormous effort. He and Laurie Lawrence had bonded well and were pushing hard towards the Commonwealth Games in Christchurch in 1974 and the Montreal Olympics in 1976.

I remember some of the remarkable training feats that Laurie and Stephen would do in an average training session. For example, on the swim clock, Steve would swim thirty fifty-metre laps, non-stop. He would dive start and hit the wall at the other end, jump out of the water, and dive start again before the swim clock had recorded thirty-five seconds. This went on for thirty laps, a truly remarkable feat. For anybody that knows anything about swimming, I am sure you would agree.

In 1973, we had been at Carina Pool for three years. Jude and I were still hard at it while Stephen was giving it his absolute best. The press had dubbed him 'super fish' after Laurie compared his two-beat kick style to the tail of a dolphin. When he competed in the Australian Championships in Brisbane, at age fifteen, Steve set a new freestyle world record swimming 1500 metres in a time of 15 minutes 34 seconds.

The press went mad, and Steve Holland became a household name. Everybody wanted a piece of him. If Steve farted, the whole world had to know about it. This victory qualified him for the 1973 World Aquatic Championships in Belgrade, Yugoslavia.

It didn't take long before the event was on our doorstep. I got Jude to show me on the world atlas where Belgrade was located, and decided that flying a distance like that was not for me. So I regrettably pulled out of the trip to Belgrade. Life at home without Jude and Steve was a very different place, and It gave me a true understanding of how many hours Jude put into making where we lived a success.

All of the kids and I watched Steve swim an amazing 1500 metres where he again set a new world record, again breaking the 800 as well on the way through. The current world record holder was an American called Rick DeMont. I will never forget Norman May from the ABC calling the race. Norman was so excited that we all felt that we were there in Belgrade. When it came to Steve finishing his last lap, Norman called his final touch at thirty laps and was cheering Steve's great feat, when out of the blue, Steve did another tumble turn and went on to swim an extra two laps. Well, that really revved up Norman's call of the race. Poor old Rick DeMont from the USA was also still swimming, chasing Steve. As Steve finished his thirty-second lap, he soon realised that he had over-swum the race; he had swum two extra laps, but had reset his world record to 15minute 31.85 seconds. DeMont got out of the pool and immediately congratulated Steve on his world championship win and then announced his retirement from competitive swimming. The crowd was going wild and Norman May was still trying to put his teeth back in after the call of his career.

Steve's next mission was to win a gold medal at the Christchurch Commonwealth Games in 1974. Jude was insistent that she and I would travel to New Zealand and watch Steve swim in the 1500 metres, and of course that meant a flight in a big jet aircraft. *Bloody hell,* I thought. I had only been on an aeroplane once in my life and that was to Sydney in an old DC3. I dared not think of how much terror would be flowing through my veins preparing for this trip. Every day that went by was another day closer. Steve had left with the Australian team to get over the ditch and prepare for his first international swim. He looked amazing in his last session at home, and he had been prepared magnificently by Laurie. I remember watching him leap out of the shallow end of the home fifty-metre pool. As he stood up and got his breath at the edge of the pool, he gave a little grin and a laugh. His stomach muscles vibrated like the pistons on a performance race car. I was, and always will be, extremely proud of Steve, not only as an athlete but as a good fun-loving boy. I also reflected on some of our whiting trips in the old fishing dinghy, me at the outboard and Allan and Steve as young kids tucked under an old piece of black plastic to keep dry; and Jude and the girls standing on Cleveland Point watching me and the boys coming home, punching our way into the late afternoon southeaster that was common at that time of the year. The piece of black plastic was a remnant of one of the black plastic pool covers that I used to help keep the heat in the teaching pool at Cannon Hill. It is true testament to the fact that the simpler you keep life, the more you get out of it.

Well, Jude and I were travelling the next day to New Zealand. The hair on the back of my neck was hot and sweaty. We had an early flight and needed to be at Eagle Farm airport at 7 am. The girls and Allan and Troy and Shona were all set up while we were away. It was now up to Jude and I to be on time and we were up and in the car by 6 am. Hugs and kisses all round.

As the taxi pulled up at the airport, I could hear the boom of a jet aeroplane roaring its way down the runway. The hairs on the back of my neck were at it again; I was numb with terror. Jude grabbed me by the hand and reassured me that all would be okay. That calmed me momentarily. We checked our luggage in and sat waiting for the call to board. The call over the loud speaker pierced my heart, and Jude had to assist me at getting to my feet.

We were greeted by some lovely air hostesses and I took a window seat. *Well*, I thought, *if there was a crash I can kick the window out and escape.* As I sat in my seat, Jude slid in beside me on the aisle. From the moment I sat down, I was feeling awful, so as one of the hosties went by I got her attention and requested a sick bag. Jude was a bit embarrassed, and she explained that this was my first trip. The hostess gave a little giggle and was quick to point out that we were still on the ground. I was quick to respond and say that the sick bag was urgent. She handed me a paper bag and told me to stay calm. *Easy words*, I thought.

As always, Jude was calm and supportive.

'Jude,' I said. 'What is that noise?'

She responded by saying that this was all new to her as well. 'I guess they have started the engines,' she said.

Well, that was it. I was vomiting uncontrollably and trying to look as inconspicuous as possible. After that, I felt a little better, and I sat back in my seat and waited for the command from the captain—'Evacuate, evacuate!' How did I get myself in such a state?

'You know Jude, I think I will swim home.'

'How far is it?'

'I am not meant to fly.'

'It's okay, Roy,' Jude reassured me again.

As I felt the plane lift off, I pushed myself to look out of the window, and the first thing I saw as we gained some height was the Redbank Meatworks in clear view on the banks of the Brisbane River. I could not help wondering who of my past co-workers were still stuck in that house of terror: Chooka Lewis, Ferpo Neuman, Billy Cummins? How did I get myself and my family to this point? Who had guided us to this point? A great family, every one of us a success and doing their best. Then it hit me: Jude was the short answer. She had dealt with the early loss of her mum, then being shipped off to a mission in Leeton in central New South Wales as a four-year-old orphan. What an amazing effort. I sometimes would have thoughts that Jude could have been Aboriginal; those thoughts started way back at Tugun Surf Club, when Jude used to come down to visit me. Some of the club members would call out, 'Hey, Roy, your little black girl is downstairs.' I would run down the stairs and she would give me a beautiful smile. I was aware Jude had experienced terrible rejection from her supposed family. Also, she did not have any childhood photographs of her or her family. I just never brought the subject up. She was totally committed to the success of our family and that was all that mattered.

So I tried to man-up a bit, and realise who I was sitting next to—a truly dynamic person, and a great example to the whole family.

It was a very exciting Commonwealth Games, and Steve won every race that he contested in New Zealand, including a world record for the 400 metres freestyle.

I decided not to swim back to Australia, and was a better traveller from that point on. Jude and I arrived back home to a barrage of press. Of course Steve got back into the pool and Jude went back to those bloody squash courts.

On our return home, the press again were relentless, and it was difficult for everybody to settle. But with the Montreal Olympics still two years away, Steve needed a break from his day to day training programs, and decided to take up an offer to travel to the USA and attend a university on a sports scholarship. That was a mistake; all it did was wake up Steve's oncoming competitors as to what volume of kilometres had to be swum in the training pool to achieve the target time of 15 minutes for 1500 metres.

It was not long before the novelty wore off in the USA and Steve was on his way back home. Steve got back into the home pool and went hard heading up to the 1976 Montreal Games. Laurie Lawrence decided that he needed a break and Steve had to find another coach. Bad timing, but that is life, and other people have to live it as well. We took up an offer from a new coach, Bill Sweetnham. He was a good swimmer and was enthusiastic about taking the reins. All went well until the swim in Montreal. Before the race, a new tactic was to be adopted. The two swimmers from the USA, Bobby Hackett and Brian Goodell, were Steve's main rivals, and were both 400 metre world class swimmers; they were faster swimmers at that distance. Steve was a long distance swimmer and his normal tactic was to take off flat out start to finish, catch me if you can approach. In any sport, if you are hurting and tired, it is hard to mount an attack on the current world record holder when he is so far in front. However, the new tactic was for Steve to start out more conservatively and make his move at the 800 metre mark. Although Steve broke his own world record down to 15.03 minutes, Hackett and Goodell moved past him with 200 metres to go. Steve picked up a bronze medal for his country. Although Steve got beaten on the day, he certainly did not disgrace himself. He also won the only individual medal for Australia at those Olympic Games. *Well done Steve,* I thought.

Again, when Steve came back home there was the usual barrage of press, only this time it was different and the whole family were disappointed for Steve. Jude and I decided to go back to Cannon Hill and re-establish our Holland Dolphin Swim School.

Then, in 1980, Jude and I bought a house at Currumbin Beach, back where it all began, just near where I took Jude on our first date all those years ago. For us, Currumbin was a wonderful twenty-odd years. We had an old house called 'the love shack' and built another beautiful house behind it with magnificent views of the beach and the coastline. We lived in the new house and all the kids could come and stay in the shack.

But, in 2000, after twenty years of climbing stairs, it was time to move back to Brisbane. The stairs had worn Jude's knees out and we were missing Brisbane. We both needed more medical care. I had a heart condition that almost took my life, and Jude was struggling with the normal day to day things that challenge you when you start getting old. We were both getting used to the fact that getting old was hard work! Allan our eldest son and Deb our middle daughter had built a pair of cojoined houses in Wynnum, a bayside suburb in Brisbane. The houses were built on Wynnum Creek. So we sold the Currumbin house, cashed up; we paid some rent and were very happy. I could fish and catch mud crabs; Jude loved mud crabs. She would bang away at them with a small hammer, and she would say, 'Roy it is like feeding strawberries to a pig, love', and give me a wonderful smile as she ripped another muddie into pieces. I was more in love with Jude than I could remember. She had put in a big effort with my reading and maths; she always protected me when spelling and maths came into my life; and I was starting to read a book.

Our only vice was playing poker machines. Jude was so clever that she could beat the machines more times than not. I, on the other hand, was not as skilful with numbers and she called me the liability. I lost more times than I won, but when I did win, she would praise me. As long as I was with her, I didn't care. On our way to our favourite club, we were like two little kids going to the lolly shop. We had started playing the pokies when we moved to Currumbin. We would go over the Queensland-New South Wales border and play the machines with some of the cash that came our way from our learn-to-swim school. We loved the pokies; neither of us drank or smoked so this was our thing, and if we both won on the night, on the way home we would be laughing and carrying on like five year olds—just loved it.

Life at Wynnum living next door to Allan was great. We moved in 2006 and had six great years. The time there was very good for Allan. He had married at nineteen, so Jude and I got to connect with him a lot more by living next door.

Plenty of family contact was good timing, because Jude was diagnosed with lung cancer. I was at my absolute lowest; the cancer was probably caused by the passive smoking that was allowed in the clubs in the early days of poker machines. All the family gathered around Jude, and she did everything possible to beat the disease. About a year after her diagnosis, she went into hospital, and unfortunately whilst she was sedated, she was left sitting on the edge of her bed. She lost her balance and fell face-first onto the concrete floor. Poor love, she was battered and bruised on her face. On the day this happened, all of our kids heard of the accident and responded. This is what happened: the seven of us, Jude and I, Allan, Jan, Deb, Steve, and Cathy were chatting together and trying to give Jude the support she needed, when a nurse came into the room, took Jude's blood pressure and found it to be quite low. 'Must be the machine,' Jude whispered we all agreed. Another machine was brought into the room and another test. No, Jude's blood pressure was dangerously low. When Jude fell asleep, a nurse of Indian descent called us all to gather around Jude. The nurse said that Jude was starting her 'next journey'. My God, Jude had left us.

From that moment forward, life was over for me. I could not go back to live at Wynnum with Allan. The house there held too many memories of Jude and myself. For the next six years I could not settle on my own, and became more unsettled and angry about being alone and on my own at almost ninety years of age. Allan wanted me to go into a care facility, where I could have more contact with other people my age, but I was not that sort of person. I took time to reflect on what Jude and I had achieved: five wonderful self-driven children, all of whom had pursued their own careers. Allan had become a successful inventor, while Jan, had created her own swim school business at Langlands Park Pool in Brisbane. Deb had moved to Currumbin in the late eighties, married John, and together established John Munro Agencies, a very successful business. Steve had the last laugh, and became a very skilful businessman establishing his own oil distribution business, And of course, little Cath had continued to own and operate the old Holland Dolphin Pool that we'd built sixty years ago in the backyard at Cannon Hill. She was doing a great job and I laughed to myself, thinking that the two girls with their own swim schools would not be charging two bob a lesson, as Jude and I did a lifetime ago!

So now as my life is coming to an end, I look back and am grateful. To my five kids, I am eternally grateful for your efforts; may you all find strength from all that has been achieved by the entire family. I also am proud of the high elbow freestyle stroke that has remained the key factor between a swimmer who can bash their way up and down the pool, and one of our swimmers who can glide their way through the water. It is 'the Holland way'. The only difference between all of our students was that some swam faster than others. Most importantly, they are all good swimmers. I am and will always be missing Jude. I am ninety in a couple of months, and I cannot see myself pushing through the depression that has silently slipped into my life since Jude and my brother Harold passed. I can hear the words of Reverend Parsons at my mum Minnie's funeral when he insisted that there is everlasting life.

Hey Jude! I am on my journey!

Afterword and acknowledgements

This story has been written in an effort to explain how we Hollands from Cannon Hill came to be where we are today. I have written this story based on memories and stories told to me by my dad, Roy. Some stories have been given a bit more depth, but generally the stories are true. Forgive me if you think some of the dates are not exactly correct; they are to the best of my memory and calculation.

Finally, it has been my pleasure to have written this story and I wish to thank both Beverley Streater and Professor Julie Dunn for their efforts in bringing the story to you.

www.ingramcontent.com/pod-product-compliance
Lightning Source LLC
Chambersburg PA
CBHW051436290426
44109CB00016B/1583